EARLY-START
POTTY
TRAINING

LINDA SONNA, PH.D.

McGraw·Hill

New York   Chicago   San Francisco   Lisbon   London   Madrid   Mexico City
Milan   New Delhi   San Juan   Seoul   Singapore   Sydney   Toronto

Library of Congress Cataloging-in-Publication Data

Sonna, Linda, 1950–
    Early-start potty training / by Linda Sonna.
        p.   cm.
    Includes bibliographical references and index.
    ISBN 0-07-145800-X (alk. paper)
    1. Toilet training.   I. Title.

    HQ770.5.S65   2005
    649'.62—dc22   2005003501

1 2 3 4 5 6 7 8 9 0   FGR/FGR   0 9 8 7 6 5

ISBN 0-07-145800-X

McGraw-Hill books are available at special quantity discounts to use as premiums and sales promotions, or for use in corporate training programs. For more information, please write to the Director of Special Sales, Professional Publishing, McGraw-Hill, Two Penn Plaza, New York, NY 10121-2298. Or contact your local bookstore.

The information contained in this book is designed for educational purposes only and is not intended to provide medical advice or other professional services. The information should not be used for diagnosis, for treatment, or as a substitute for professional care. If your child has a medical or behavioral problem or you suspect such a possibility, consult your health-care provider. All case studies are composites designed to reflect common behaviors and situations. Information has been changed to protect parents' and children's identities.

This book is printed on acid-free paper.

To my foster children and grandchildren:
Thanks for the many lessons in how to potty train!

Contents

Foreword

About a dozen years ago, during a routine well baby exam, I had an experience that altered my thinking on potty training. I asked the adorable baby girl's mother about the child's development. "She's fine," the mother answered. "She coos, turns her head to my voice, and reaches out and grabs for objects. She can lift her head high, smile, and laugh. A delightfully normal baby." She paused. "And she is toilet trained," the mom added quietly.

"Excuse me?" I responded.

"She is toilet trained."

I did not comprehend what she was saying about this precious eleven-pound cutie. "What do you mean?" I asked.

The mom explained patiently, and as if I were the most idiotic physician she had ever encountered, "She uses the toilet: she pees and poops on a toilet." Well, this was a four-month-old and I knew she could sit only with support, so the idea of this darling baby sitting on a toilet fit nowhere in my visual imagination.

It is not proper to contradict a parent directly, but I just could not imagine a toilet-trained infant. I replied, "I have never heard of a toilet-trained four-month-old. I would be very curious to see how that works."

Mom proposed a demonstration, using the plastic "barf bucket" basin from the exam room cabinet. She removed the child's diaper, perched her little bottom over the edge of the basin, and sort of hissed softly "psssst psssst psssst" at the little baby. Within seconds the child began to urinate into the basin. I was speechless. Mom patted her little bum with a tissue and replaced the dry diaper. Then she very kindly explained that her family was from China, where disposable diapers and handy washing machines were not common. She began to place the infant on the edge of the toilet around fifteen days of age, and now at four months, she used only one diaper per day!

After the experience with the four-month-old, I have come to believe that what we actually do is *train* our infants to go potty in their diapers. Being christened by a urinating bare-bottomed newborn is almost a rite of passage of parenthood. By several months of age, it is less common for a naked baby to go. Many parents can recall an experience of removing a well-used diaper, cleaning up the baby's bottom, and putting a clean replacement diaper around the infant, only to have the child instantly pee or poop into the new diaper, as if he or she was just waiting for the cleanup before the next "job" could be produced.

Eureka! That's it! We start training our babies to go potty in their diapers from the first few minutes of life. Our brilliant new-borns quickly learn that if they go without a diaper, we jump back, squeal, and make horrible faces. They learn within a few months that they need to go in the diaper to avoid the unpleasant reaction of their caregiver.

What if toilet training was just another skill that infants learned? What if we thought of it like learning that the tub was for bathing, the high chair was for eating, and the car seat was for traveling? We don't wait until our children ask or give clues that they are ready for a bath or for a ride in the car. We *teach* them that these activities, which are a part of everyone's daily life, occur in a specific place. We don't make a big deal out of these places: tubs, car seats, highchairs. Why in the world do we make such a big deal about using the toilet? Why do we wait until the more difficult toddler years, when our children prefer familiar routines, familiar foods, familiar people, familiar places, to introduce a new activity—using the toilet? Why do we force our infants to learn to tolerate being wrapped in their own body waste? Not even our hamsters, puppies, or kittens tolerate that!

What if toilet training was approached as a skill, like rolling over, sitting, and walking? We can give our babies opportunities to practice toilet sitting, just like tummy time to practice rolling over or floor time to practice crawling. The physiologic ability to begin to control the muscles involved in controlling urination and bowel movements should occur around five to nine months, around the time the baby can sit unsupported. After that, it's a matter of perfecting the new skill, which just takes lots of practice. It's not magic, it's not psychology, and it's not a trick. It's just a motor skill that your baby needs to have an opportunity to practice.

Dr. Sonna is giving parents and babies a wonderful opportunity to introduce the potty at an age when learning new skills is part of everyday life. Your baby is ready to learn every day. You present life experiences every day to your baby. This can be just another of life's expectations, rather than a huge burdensome project with a stubborn toddler. I commend her on her endeavor to share this approach with the parents of the twenty-first century. Best wishes to the parents and babies for this mission!

—*Barbara Gablehouse, M.D., F.A.A.P.*

Preface

After my first potty-training book was published in 2003, e-mails from desperate parents began flooding in. Their stories were remarkably similar. The parents had begun working with their children around age three and avoided pressuring them to learn or criticizing them for accidents, yet training limped along in fits and starts. At age four, five, and six, their youngsters continued to have one or more difficulties:

- Children had accidents within minutes of saying they didn't need to use the potty.
- Children would use the potty to pee or poop but not for both.
- Children insisted on standing to have bowel movements.
- Children did not mind the smell or feel of wet and soiled clothing.
- Children had accidents soon after long potty sits.
- Children wet the bed despite being basically trained.

I began combing through medical journals for solutions and was amazed to find that slow potty-training progress and chronic toileting problems are known to be related to starting to potty train after age two, wearing disposable diapers, and failing to take the child to the potty regularly. Why, I wondered, do most pediatricians advocate starting to train after age two? Why aren't parents being warned that disposable diapers make it hard for children to learn? Why do authors of potty-training books and articles routinely say parents should use a hands-off approach and let children lead the way?

After researching the matter further, it began to seem that the standard recommendations from professionals rest on a single forty-year-old study conducted by the paid spokesman for Pampers disposable diapers. That study was too flawed to yield any trustworthy conclusions. I couldn't imagine why professionals were ignoring the numerous well-done studies, some of which are listed in the Endnotes.

I went from thinking that professionals weren't bothering to read the research to imagining some sort of grand conspiracy designed to keep children in diapers for years on end. But when I sat down to write this book, I understood why professionals might be hesitant to let the public know that even infants and babies can be potty trained and that structure and limits make it easier for toddlers to learn. Potty-training accidents are already the second leading factor in child abuse. Even mild criticism and punishment slows potty training and can result in long-term problems. I wasn't sure the average parent could understand the difference between being firm and being harsh.

In the end, I decided that parents deserve accurate information. They need to know that early potty training is important for bladder health. At the same time, they must understand that forcing children to use the potty is impossible and trying can seriously backfire. The challenge is to get children to the potty consistently at the right times and teach them to sit quietly and relax without pressuring them to produce and perform. Setting kind, consistent limits and knowing when to back off are invaluable parenting skills. Once mastered, they can readily be applied to other child-rearing issues. Doing so will make for healthier, happier children all around.

Acknowledgments

Laurie Boucke, Reno Lovison, Kathleen Knoth, Lois Sonna, Peter Rubie, John Aherne, "Mema" of Mema's Child Care, Mary Gugino, Michele Gia, Dr. Larry Sonna, Denise Kunesh, Cynthia Holmire, Ingrid Bauer, Dr. Sarah Buckley, Phyllis Braun, Mark Sonna, Karol Seay, Dr. Alden Cockburn, and Margie Henzel. Special thanks to research assistant and editor Lyn Bleiler for her extensive contributions.

1

All Aboard!

Speeding Your Child's Journey

"Still he wears diapers?" Jessica's mother-in-law asked in her heavy Russian accent. She clucked while stroking her grandson's head. "Poor little malysh. Back in my country . . ."

Jessica's eyes glazed over. Here we go again, she thought. She was tired of the not-so-subtle hints to start potty training. Jessica didn't know what to think about her mother-in-law's boast that her four kids had been potty trained by age eighteen months. Jessica had a hard time believing it was true. All the books and articles she had read said that children simply didn't have enough muscle control until much later. They needed to be emotionally ready, too. On a Pampers ad, a famous pediatrician said, "Don't rush your toddler into toilet training or let anyone else tell you it's time! It's got to be his choice!" In truth, his advice didn't make sense to Jessica, either. How could two-year-olds make intelligent choices when they didn't know anything about the subject?

Jessica dreaded having to tackle the project of potty training her son. But given the problems with diaper rash, the high cost of diapers, and the mountains of laundry, she would gladly start today if she could be sure he was ready. But how to tell?

If you are like most parents, your number-one question about potty training is when to begin. The answer may come as a surprise: the best time to begin potty training is *now*!

Understanding how the body works and mastering toileting skills is a tall order for small humans who have only recently arrived on the planet. Potty-training experts are on target when they urge parents to think in terms of "toilet learning" rather than "toilet training." Teaching is simple and straightforward, and every child does learn. But learning takes time.

Most parents find it hard to believe that it is better to get their child on board the potty train sooner than later or that the present moment is the best time to begin. "But what about potty-training readiness?" a mother asks. "I read that it's important to wait until a child shows an interest in learning," a father insists. Indeed, most books and articles urge parents to wait . . . and wait . . . and wait.

The notion that later is better has been pushed by pediatric spokesmen for the multibillion-dollar disposable-diaper industry since the 1960s. Soon after, most pediatricians and child-guidance experts echoed the recommendation to wait until after age two. By suggesting that early learning can cause psychological damage and years of toileting problems, the experts convinced parents that it is harmful.

Delaying has been a boon for the corporate bottom line. It has also turned what was once a natural learning process into a stressful, frustrating, and expensive nightmare for countless families. In 1961, before disposables flooded the marketplace, 90 percent of children were potty trained by age two and a half years. In 1998, that figure dropped to just 22 percent. In 2001, according to a study reported in *Ambulatory Pediatrics*, the average age for completing potty training rose to thirty-five months for girls and thirty-nine months for boys. It is no longer uncommon for children ages four, five, and even six to wear diapers, despite the fact that children have enough physical control to begin the

> **Quick Trip**
> The principal research studies and source materials used to for-
> mulate recommendations for *Early-Start Potty Training* appear
> in the Endnotes near the back of this book. If you want to do
> some technical research of your own, a good place to begin is
> with Wilhelmina Bakker's *Research into the Influence of Potty-
> Training on Lower Urinary Tract Dysfunction* (Belgium: Univer-
> sity of Antwerp, 2002). To obtain a copy of this comprehensive
> work, check with a university interlibrary loan program.

potty-training process at age three months. But that's not what
the so-called experts are saying. The reason, according to toilet-
training researcher Timothy R. Schum, is that ". . . most advice
on this topic is based on theory and common experience rather
than on scientific knowledge." (See Endnotes.) That "common
experience" is actually limited to a small group of Western
countries.

Traditional Schedules

The truth about the ability of young toddlers and babies to learn
to use the potty may be one of the best-kept secrets in America.
Even as millions of U.S. parents anxiously watch for signs that
their three-and-a-half-year-old has attained a mysterious state of
readiness so they can begin teaching, parents in other countries
have tossed the diaper rash cream, hauled the changing table up
to the attic, and found another use for the diaper bag.

Parents in most of the rest of the world put babies on small potties for short periods of time as soon as they can sit up by themselves. By making the time spent on the potty enjoyable, parents

help the youngsters overcome any fear they might have of the toilet. Parents reward their babies' occasional successes with smiles and applause, which delights little ones even if they don't understand what all the excitement is about. Over time, they come to accept potty time as readily as mealtime, naptime, bath time, and bedtime. As soon as they can toddle about the house on their own two legs, their parents steer them to the potty for regular practice sessions. When they master the mechanics of buttons and zippers so they can get their clothes off and back on by themselves, they are fully trained. As a result, most toddlers around the globe finish training by ages eighteen to twenty-four months.

Moreover, a review of past potty-training timetables shows that waiting until babies can sit up by themselves might actually be very *late*! Incredible as it now seems, in the early 1900s, U.S. parents managed infant waste with minimal use of diapers. The favored technique was to position little handheld pots under a newborn and make a special sound when the youngster eliminated. Over time, infants became conditioned to the special sound and feel of the pot touching their bottoms. When that happened, they responded by pushing to relieve themselves. The national pediatric debate at the time centered on whether parents should have infants board the potty train at age two *months* or to allow them an extra month to mature before starting their journey.

When automatic washing machines ended the drudgery of laundering cloth diapers in the 1940s, infant training went the way of the steam engine in industrialized nations. Because washing diapers was no longer so difficult, parents began waiting to introduce the potty until babies could sit up by themselves. Still, the norm was for children to finish training by ages one and a half to two. In 1946, Dr. Benjamin Spock wrote the first edition of *The Pocket Book of Baby and Child Care*, which became the child-rearing bible for the next generation of U.S. parents. His extremely liberal, child-centered views shocked the nation. He

> **Quick Trip**
> Whether you're gooing at your infant, gurgling at your baby, talk-ing to your toddler, or prattling with your preschooler, start teaching the concepts of wet and dry today. Repeat the words *wet* and *dry* while touching your child's hand to wet and dry diapers, washcloths, sponges, dishrags, socks, or towels so he can feel the difference.

recommended waiting to put children onto the potty until age seven to nine months. U.S. parents responded en masse, and in 1957 "only" half began training by age nine months.

Putting on the Brakes

As Procter & Gamble began test-marketing the first disposable diapers in 1961, the company searched for a pediatrician to pro-mote them. It signed up T. Berry Brazelton, who began extolling the merits of the company's product and recommending that parents not begin potty training before children are physi-cally, mentally, and emotionally ready. The professor-turned-infomercial-star pointed out that with a more mature, verbal youngster for a traveling companion, the route to continence was destined to be less bumpy and more direct. Families could avoid the many missed connections that make working with younger tots a bit tricky, arrive at the final destination at about the same time, and avoid long-term problems with wetting and soiling. His "child-oriented" approach centered around not starting to teach until the youngster wanted to learn—and backing off immedi-ately if an initially eager tot grew bored with the project or had a change of heart.

> **Quick Trip**
> Disposable diapers eliminate the sensation of wetness. That makes it hard for children to relate the sensations of needing to eliminate with wetting and soiling, which slows potty training. On average, youngsters clad in cloth finish potty training a year *earlier*. Ditch the disposables, and voilà: your child is on board the potty train.

Ironically, Brazelton's own study of mothers whom he personally "liberated" from early training was too poorly done to draw any conclusions but suggested some potentially serious drawbacks to late training. His findings, which appeared in *Pediatrics* in 1962, showed that one-third of children who didn't stop wetting the bed until age three and a half had started training early. But viewed from that perspective, two-thirds of the children who didn't stop wetting the bed until age three and a half were late starters, and most had begun training at twenty-four months. And, of the children who continued to wet and soil after age five, only 12.5 percent had started training before eighteen months of age. The vast majority (87.5 percent) had started training after twenty-four months of age. Nevertheless, in countless Pampers ads and through his position as head of the Pampers Institute, Brazelton reiterated his certainty that it was better to leave potty-training decisions to the whims of each child. It's no surprise that disposable diaper sales began to soar.

Derailed!

The fear that early training was psychologically harmful and the ease of disposables induced parents to swaddle their tots in paper and start training later. When they finally left the station, some were able to potty train in short order. But many arrived much later than expected after a long, harrowing ride.

Once the "terrible twos" passed, experts said the potty-training journey should be amazingly swift and smooth. Indeed, many older toddlers prove to be eager, highly capable students. "One day my child seemed ready. A week later he was trained!" countless parents have proclaimed. However, many other parents find their child has been derailed. "One day my child seemed ready. Years later, he still wasn't trained," many parents complain.

It's not surprising that when children start training between ages two and three, many have such slow learning curves. Youngsters in this age group are famous for their contrariness. Once terribly two-year-old types are old enough to just say no, inducing them to say yes to much of anything is difficult. Getting them to relax while doing something they don't want to do—a basic requirement for potty training—is even harder. After the novelty of sitting on a shiny new potty wears off, many tykes simply refuse to hold still for the ride. Starting potty training between ages two and three increases the likelihood of parent-child conflict, and when parents try to force the issue, potty training stalls.

The smell of an untrained preschool or kindergarten student can draw very negative reactions from peers, and after being stigmatized and shunned, many youngsters vow to reach the potty-training finish line ASAP. Unfortunately, large numbers are unable to do so. If children do not start learning until around age three, they often face a number of special problems:

- Long-established habits of using the diaper as a toilet are entrenched.
- After having ignored the sensations related to elimination for so many years, many youngsters seem to have great difficulty identifying them.

- After passing waste while walking about in diapers for so many years, many children have difficulty figuring out how to work their muscles while sitting down.
- Over half of children ages three and up have occasional or chronic problems with constipation. A single bout during potty training can lead to resistance, refusals, and chronic toileting problems.

Nevertheless, Brazelton applauds parents for waiting, viewing their willingness to allow youngsters to wet and soil themselves for a couple of extra years as a sign of respect for their bodies. To accommodate them, Brazelton recommends Procter & Gamble's latest edition to the Pampers line: size 6.

And now the timetable is being pushed back even further. Some pediatricians suggest that it is fine to wait until age four or four and a half before beginning potty training. That means most families will soon need many more than the current average of six to eight thousand diapers per child. To accommodate the crowds of older passengers, companies are cranking out disposable diapers and pull-up training pants in jumbo and mega sizes.

Quick Trip

Change your toddler's diapers at least once every two hours. Once youngsters become accustomed to the smell and feel of wet and soiled diapers, they have less incentive to learn to use the potty. Tots need to be allowed to spend time naked from the waist down so they can begin learning the most basic fact of all: pee and poop come from their own body. Youngsters who wear diapers 24/7 don't even know that!

On the Wrong Track

The American Academy of Pediatrics "Toilet Training Readiness" Web page displays an amazing ignorance of children's bodies. It states, "Children younger than 12 months have no control over bladder or bowel movements and little control for 6 months or so after that. Between 18 and 24 months, children often start to show signs of being ready, but some children may not be ready until 30 months or older."

It is hard to fathom how America's most eminent pediatricians arrived at their conclusions. Apparently the authors of the official U.S. toilet-training guidelines haven't been reading their organization's journal. A 1994 study in the *Journal of Developmental and Behavioral Pediatrics* found no data to support any specific signs of social or emotional readiness for potty training. Apparently the doctors who wrote the official U.S. guidelines never discussed the matter with their own parents or grandparents to see how they managed to train young toddlers in the days before disposable products. A trip to Eastern Europe, Africa, the Orient, or Latin America would confirm that most of the world's parents use loving, humane methods to help infants and babies communicate their elimination needs to avoid accidents.

If a journey to a far-off land is too difficult, skeptics need only make a quick trip to the southern U.S. border to set the record straight. Convince an impoverished Mexican *mamacita* to extricate a naked infant from the folds of her *rebozo* shawl, and a two-second touch-and-sniff test will confirm the truth. A dry shawl free of telltale bathroom odors proves the capabilities of tiny babies: early potty training does work. Moreover, there is no indication that early training causes children to develop toileting problems later in life. My interviews with a nonrandom smattering of Mexican moms suggest that their older kids are doing fine.

> **Quick Trip**
> It's "monkey see, monkey do" in the toddler world, and young-sters with a potty-trained older sibling or day-care pal learn to use the potty sooner. If no older child is willing to serve as a role model, start inviting your youngster to join you for a look-see when you use the toilet. To cope with the assault on your privacy, spend the moments envisioning how you will spend your time once you are liberated from diaper drudgeries.

Dangerous Crossings

If having to cope with preschoolers and kindergarteners in dia-pers is hard on caregivers, youngsters who end up wearing dia-pers for years on end clearly suffer most of all. Contrary to what television ads have led parents to believe, disposables do *not* keep children "clean and dry." They keep them filthy and dry. Diaper rash, a disorder that was once a telling sign of parental neglect, used to affect about 7 percent of babies. Now that 94 percent of children wear disposables, diaper rash afflicts 78 percent. Having children "wear their waste" for years on end is a definite health hazard. In fact, most of the illnesses that rage through day-care centers and nurseries these days are caused by *E. coli*, the bacte-ria from fecal contamination. Giardia and rotavirus are also spread through human waste.

Infection may prove to be the least of children's diaper-related problems. The chemicals used to manufacture disposable diapers also leak from wet diapers and are absorbed through the skin. When changing diapers, parents commonly find globs of the superabsorbent gel on their children's genitals. Many parents report allergic reactions, and some say that disposables have triggered asthma attacks in susceptible children. Such clinical reports have not been confirmed by laboratory studies. However, breathing the fumes from an open box of disposable diapers has been shown to decrease airflow and cause lung irritation in laboratory mice. Rosin compounds were identified in all disposable diapers tested by Swedish researchers, the highest amounts being in the diapers produced by the two leading manufacturers. Rosin has been known to cause dermatitis in sensitive children.

The rise of male infertility and increased incidence of undescended testicles in little boys have coincided with the widespread use of disposables. A team of researchers believes that disposable diapers may play a role. By containing body heat along with the drips and puddles, disposables raise the temperature of the testicles and scrotum. Prolonged temperature elevation during childhood has been associated with infertility later in life.

Delaying potty training is also associated with more frequent urination and can result in other health problems. Because children don't routinely push when peeing until they are being potty trained, they do not exercise their muscles and may not completely empty the bladder. The results of not fully emptying the bladder range from chronic infections to unstable bladders. The former can even lead to scarring of the kidneys. For the latter,

Quick Trip

Wash your baby's hands after each potty use. Learning the rituals required for proper hygiene is an essential part of toileting. Wash your own hands as well. Many digestive ailments and bouts of diarrhea that parents think are symptoms of the flu or food poisoning are actually the result of infection from fecal contamination.

the bladder contractions needed to expel urine are too strong, too weak, or occur unexpectedly, leading to accidents. Urinating voluntarily uses the pelvic floor muscles and helps maintain muscle awareness and strength. The pelvic floor muscles are important for continence in later life.

The Window Seat

Late training also takes a tremendous toll on the environment. Hundreds of thousands of trees are used to make the sixteen billion disposable diapers U.S. children use each year. A by-product of the manufacturing process, dioxin, is a carcinogen. Dioxin causes cancer, nerve damage, and a host of other physical ills. Greenpeace in Europe, an environmental organization, has found organotins in Procter & Gamble's Pampers and Pampers Baby Dry Mini (in the adhesive belt area), and in Fixies Ultra Dry disposable diapers. These toxic chemical compounds are frequently used in the superabsorbent gel in disposable diapers. Greenpeace has demanded a worldwide ban of organotins in all products. Organotins have been found to harm the immune system and have been deemed responsible for toxic shock syndrome suffered

Quick Trip

Rather than interrupt their play for a potty trip, toddlers who are in the process of potty training may use their diaper as a toilet or try to "hold it." Diapers are unsanitary; "holding it" for too long can stretch the bladder and increase the risk of infection. Teach your child that Mother Nature's call must be answered immediately, not ignored or put on hold.

by women wearing tampons. Researchers at Murray State University in Kentucky found that one hour of lab exposure to "environmentally relevant levels" of an organotin known as tributyltin inhibited the "tumor killing ability of natural killer cells."

Disposable diapers are now the third leading component of the nation's landfills (behind newspapers and discarded fast-food and beverage containers). And since discarded diapers contain untreated waste, astronomical quantities of raw sewage are dumped into the earth. Then there is the energy that is used to manufacture disposables and to launder cloth diapers. The chemicals used to clean and sanitize cloth diapers pollute rivers and streams. So, early training is a definite plus for the environment.

Early Departures

Now that so many Western parents are struggling with untrained older children, interest in time-honored, natural infant-hygiene techniques is on the rise. Author Laurie Boucke's book *Infant Potty Training: A Gentle and Primeval Method Adapted to Modern Living* has been endorsed by such heavyweights as pediatrician Dr. William Sears. Boucke reports a surge in interest in these gentle, natural methods. Negative experiences with getting one of their brood out of diapers has propelled many parents to search for better training methods for subsequent children.

Best-selling author, national columnist, and family therapist John Rosemond has responded to the epidemic of wetting and soiling among older children by recommending a return to the age-old practice of potty training newly mobile tots. He points out that early learning does not turn children into emotional basket cases, scar them psychologically, or lead to years of bedwetting and accidents, as Brazelton suggests. Harsh, insensitive training methods do that.

Parents would do themselves, their children, and the environment a big favor by following the schedule that worked in the United States from the beginning of time until Pampers hit the market in 1961—and that remains so popular throughout most of the world. The primary consideration in selecting a departure date should be your personal readiness for the journey. You have plenty of choices.

• **Are you ready for infant training (zero to six months)?** Doing without diapers altogether is a demanding full-time job, if wonderfully rewarding. But even occasional use of some of the infant-training techniques can make for a better infant-parent relationship—and a happier potty-training experience down the line.

• **Are you ready for baby training (six months to eighteen months)?** You must set aside time for daily games of patty-cake or "Sooo Big!" while your youngster sits on a little potty. Babies must be able to sit upright for five to ten minutes at a stretch without teetering, tiring, toppling, or being propped.

• **Are you ready for toddler training (eighteen months to two years)?** You must provide instruction, get your tot to the bathroom every couple of hours, and respond to accidents until your child can use the potty without help.

• **Are you ready for preschooler training (two years and up)?** You must provide instruction, deliver hefty doses of encouragement and support, give prompts and reminders, and consistently respond to accidents.

Some young passengers are more eager than others to jump aboard the potty train and leave the familiar land of diapers. Some travel express down a single, nonstop route, while others need more time to absorb the lessons during what to them is a strange new journey. The good news is that everyone does arrive eventually. Teaching your child to use the potty is like any other aspect of child-rearing. Have fun when you can, keep your cool at all times, provide lots of opportunities for practice, and sooner or later your tot will learn. Here's hoping it's sooner!

Question and Answer

My neighbor swears by the "no-pressure" approach. She didn't start until her three-year-old son wanted to learn. He was completely potty trained in a week. Isn't it better to wait and let kids learn when they're ready?

Many older toddlers and preschool children do learn very quickly, and their delighted parents broadcast news of their success. Parents may be reluctant to talk about a child who started potty training at age three and required a year or two to finish. A number of long-term toileting problems are associated with starting training late and failing to provide clear, consistent structure. Every child is different, but to speed training and minimize health problems, the best bet is to start training before age two and take children to the potty regularly so they can learn.

2

Many Different Roads

Choosing Healthy Travel Routes

When Pam's parents arrived from Houston, they kissed their two-year-old grandson and stretched out their arms for their new grandbaby. "Where's my little Crystal?" Pam's mother asked. "I can't wait to see her!"

Pam quickly handed her three-week-old baby to her beaming grandmother. "But what's this?" she asked. "Crystal doesn't have any clothes on."

"Here," Pam said, handing her a diaper to tuck beneath Crystal's bottom. "To protect your clothes just in case."

"What do you mean 'just in case'?" Pam's mother demanded.

"In case of an accident."

"Surely you don't let her go around naked!"

"Not in public. But I'm potty training her, and in the privacy of our own home—"

"But her brother can see her!" Pam's mother said.

Pam tried to contain her irritation. Her mother had been so eager to see her granddaughter, but she obviously only wanted to see selected parts of her.

Pam's father jumped into the conversation to try to calm them down. "It's mighty warm in here. The kid is probably more comfortable this way. Am I right?" he asked his wife. He turned to Pam. "Probably it's a new way mothers are doing things these days. Am I right?"

Pam nodded. "Right, Dad. In fact, if you unbutton your shirt and hold her against your chest, you'll see why it's better for Crystal to be naked."

"Sure," her father said amiably. He unbuttoned his shirt, and Pam placed the baby in his arms. "Nice. Real nice," he said, holding her awkwardly against his grizzled chest. He was a dear, but he wasn't much good with infants. He always said, "I like kids when they can tell me what's on their mind so I can get to know them. Until then, they're just cute, little slobbery blobs." His words always made people laugh, but Pam knew that summed up his opinion of babies.

Later, Pam saw her dad dozing on the couch, holding his naked grandbaby while her empty carrier sat nearby. Something about the utter tenderness with which he held her, and something about the way Crystal lay snuggled in his arms, brought a lump to Pam's throat. This cuddle might have started with skin pressed to skin, but it led to some deeper connection of heart pressed to heart.

Pam saw Crystal give a little kick, her signal that she was about to pee. Her grandfather roused. "You'd better hand her to me, Dad, or you'll soon known the true meaning of 'slobbery blob,'" Pam said, hurrying the potty bowl to her daughter.

"What a thing to say!" Pam's dad protested. He actually looked indignant. "She's my precious little angel. A little angel. Am I right?" He gazed lovingly at Crystal.

"Yes, Dad," Pam said, delighted that he had bonded with his grandchild. "You're right!"

Notions about potty training have changed dramatically over the last century, and it is time to rethink them again. The standard recommendation from modern pediatricians and psychologists is to wait to begin training until close to age three for girls and a few months later for boys. If a child doesn't want to learn, parents are supposed to back off and trust that their youngster will eventually change his mind. It is considered ideal to adopt a hands-off approach and let the youngster dictate every aspect of training. Toddlers and preschool children are supposed to call the shots, drop the ball at will, and put the game on indefinite hold if they choose. Until they decide to proceed, they wear diapers or pull-up training pants 24/7. There are a number of problems with these practices:

- Parents neglect children's need for proper hygiene.
- Parents try to sell children on using the potty before they are old enough to make reasoned decisions.
- Parents send negative messages about elimination and the human body.
- Parents start training when teaching and learning about the potty are especially difficult.

Recommendations about how and when to potty train are at odds with toilet-training-research findings about what is best. For instance, most children do better with highly involved, hands-on teachers. The popularity of the hands-off approach to potty training may reflect the widespread belief among U.S. parents that elimination and sexuality are somehow linked.

The idea that potty training affects children's sexual development can make training a bit unnerving. It is understandable that so many parents dread the project and overreact to small setbacks and problems. Correcting mistaken beliefs about potty training and sexuality can go a long way toward making the project a more positive experience for both of you. It can also point the way to helping your child develop healthy attitudes toward elimination and better self-esteem.

Quick Trip

Your childhood experiences and the attitudes you absorbed from the larger culture affect how you potty train your child. Once you examine them more closely, you will probably feel more relaxed about potty training. You will be in a better position to decide what you want to pass on to your child and how to go about instilling positive attitudes toward the human body.

Victorian Teachings

The idea that natural bodily functions are sinful is a legacy from the Victorians. This Protestant group made an indelible mark on Western European culture in the 1800s. To this day, the vast majority of U.S. parents manage their children's elimination in a manner that fits neatly with Victorian aims and agendas. Members of U.S. minority groups may not share blood ties to nineteenth-century Western Europeans who crossed the Atlantic and arrived in America. But the Victorians' religious beliefs, values, and customs quickly spread from sea to shining sea.

The Victorians' deeply held religious convictions led them to spurn the human body at every turn. God-fearing Christians avoided contact with bodily flesh and juices except as required to eat, eliminate, wash, and reproduce. Cleanliness, the Calvinists believed, was next to godliness, but they weren't referring to bathing and housekeeping. Rather, they viewed the human body as inherently unclean. With their taint of original sin, infants were no better. Many modern preachers still deliver the "flesh equals sin" message to their congregations. Naked infants, bare-bottomed babies, and half-clad toddlers strike most people as somehow wrong.

Although babies' sexual organs are at least a dozen years from being fully functional, most parents are intent on keeping their children's bottoms covered. To thwart youngsters who persist in removing their diaper, moms and dads rig elaborate enclosures and deliver stern "no-no's." Many think that a young child's love of scampering about the house in his birthday suit is an early sign of exhibitionism that, if left unchecked, can lead to sexual deviance and perversion in adult life. When naked, children can more easily touch their genitals, and they do it more often. Many parents find this disturbing and insist that youngsters remain clothed. But a child's love of being naked is normal.

Diapers are bulky and confining, and many children object to wearing them. The fact that your youngster's legs are forced into an unnatural position by a lump of fabric or paper may seem like a small price for preserving modesty—assuming you have considered the matter at all. Most parents don't stop to think that diapers might be uncomfortable until their toddler manages to wiggle out of them, runs joyously naked through the house, and has a fit about being redressed.

- Your child only spends about thirty minutes a day eliminating and bathing—at most. There is no need for him to wear diapers the other twenty-three and a half hours a day.
- As soon as your child eliminates, remove the diaper and clean him up. Wait to put on a fresh diaper until it is close to time for him to eliminate again.

Instilling Positive Attitudes

Helping children develop positive attitudes toward the body is important. Although most modern parents seem to want to do this, attitudes passed to them from previous generations may interfere. The Victorians viewed female sexuality as especially voracious, intense, and tempting for hapless males. Hence, the female body was believed to be particularly dangerous for anyone who hoped that on arriving at the pearly gates, St. Peter might invite them in.

Today, parents are noticeably more tentative about touching little girls' genitals during baths and diaper changes. Boys would seem to merit more careful handling, since their primary sex organ lies outside the body, while that of little girls is safely tucked within. After a soiled diaper is removed, the average boy is scrubbed clean and rubbed dry, while his female counterpart receives a few dainty dabs and gentle pats. Parents spend more time touching the penis than the vaginal opening and clitoris. Studies show that the differences in the way youngsters are touched continues throughout childhood, causing many experts in human sexuality to believe that these differences help explain girls' lower self-esteem and difficulties feeling good about their bodies.

The main way that parents discourage children from developing positive attitudes toward the body is by covering them with a diaper and not touching them except during diaper changes and baths. That teaches them that this area of the body is only to be touched when it needs to be cleaned. Even if you refrain from shaming your toddler for accidents during potty training, swaddling your child in diapers communicates rejection of the genital area.

Keeping your child's bottom carefully concealed can send a nonverbal message that is more powerful than words. During potty training, some older toddlers and preschool children exhibit deep shame reactions. They retreat to corners or hide behind couches to eliminate unseen because they cannot bear to have anyone observe them peeing or pooping, including their parents. Some youngsters are too embarrassed to admit when they need to use the potty. This is true even though they were never punished or shamed for eliminating or having accidents.

When parents who are ashamed to have their child see them using the toilet keep the bathroom door closed, they may pass on negative attitudes toward elimination. Because their child lacks a role model, potty training progress is slower. Studies have found that firstborn children take significantly longer to learn than other youngsters, who often learn from an older sibling. Even if parents do invite their youngster into the bathroom for demonstrations, their discomfort can lead a sensitive child to conclude that something bad is happening. By age four, most children have concluded that it is. They giggle nervously while exchanging potty jokes. Despite parents' efforts to instill healthy attitudes toward elimination and the human body through pep talks, they routinely fail. Parents commonly blame peers for their child's "potty mouth," not realizing how their own attitudes and actions have influenced their youngster.

Keeping your child's bottom covered, only touching the genital area during diaper changes and baths, and criticizing your toddler for running naked through the house all communicate rejection of your child's body and contribute to the idea that it is shameful. To help your child develop a healthier attitude, remove the diaper barrier that keeps her genitals hidden after she eliminates. Clean her up and allow her to spend some time naked

Quick Trip

Leave the bathroom door open when you use the toilet so your youngster doesn't worry about what is going on or conclude that it is something too terrible for him to see. Older toddlers and preschool children need role models to demonstrate how the toilet is used. Invite your child to join you in the bathroom so he can learn the mechanics of using the toilet by watching.

before redressing her. Minimizing the time spent in diapers adds to your youngster's comfort, promotes freedom of movement of the legs, reduces exposure to the chemicals in diapers, and gives her a chance to get to know her body.

Freud's Theory

Sigmund Freud's theory of children's sexuality caused him to be written off as a sex-crazed quack in his day. His belief that children were sexual and viewed potty training as something sexual permeated the national consciousness. It struck fear in the hearts of parents and made potty training a very worrisome affair. After extensive research, Freud's theory was written off by psychologists and psychiatrists. Yet most people who haven't studied Freud in depth, which includes most parents and pediatricians, still think potty training poses a threat to a child's sexuality. Improper potty training is widely believed to lead to all sorts of sexual and personality problems in adult life.

Freud reasoned that because pee emerges from the body so close to the genitals—from the penis, in the case of boys—elimination is linked to sexuality in the minds and hearts of little children. He believed that being too lax during potty training made children forever messy. Being too strict could lead them to develop phobias about dirt and a crippling need for order. His warnings are echoed by people in everyday life as they suggest that personality quirks are due to the way they were potty trained.

Today, pediatricians seem to share the view that potty training is an extremely delicate matter, that it is somehow perceived by children as sexual, and that youngsters can be permanently scarred if their parents are displeased about accidents. Noted pediatrician T. Berry Brazelton goes so far as to urge parents to

> **Quick Trip**
>
> Becoming suddenly tentative about removing your child's diaper for potty training is likely to heighten your youngster's fear that something strange is about to happen. A more sensible approach is simply to tell your toddler you are going to teach him about peeing and pooping and explain that you are removing his diaper so he can see when it happens. You may feel that you are violating a sexual taboo when you potty train, but you are not. Elimination and sexuality are not the same.

ask permission to remove their child's diaper for potty-training purposes and to retreat if their youngster declines. Parents are told to ask if their child needs to use the potty. They are not supposed to tell their youngster to go, even when they can clearly see the signs that suggest he needs to. But of course parents constantly change diapers without asking permission. Suggesting that they ask their child's permission during potty training intimates that parents must walk on eggshells so as not to inflict psychological damage.

In actuality, potty training does not pose any special risk to children's psyches. Teaching youngsters to use the potty is like teaching them to do most anything else. They need to be shown what to do and how to do it. Most toddlers need limits to make sure they put aside other activities and go to the bathroom when instructed. And parental displeasure with accidents will not scar a child for life and can teach about the importance of cleanliness. Harsh treatment of children is uncalled for and can traumatize them regardless of the issue; there is nothing special about potty training.

Behavioral Psychology

Back in the early 1900s, parents' and pediatricians' priority was to protect children's physical health. The mortality rate among infants, babies, and toddlers was very high. Helping them survive was a challenge. Physicians believed that getting youngsters onto a schedule was important for regulating their systems. Parents were urged to keep infants on schedules for everything—eating, sleeping, and even cuddling. Being on a regular schedule also made it easier for parents to care for them, which helped with potty training when the time came.

It was known that babies can delay peeing and pooping for short periods at the age of three months, so parents understood that little ones possessed the physical control needed for potty training. Behavioral psychology explained why the techniques parents used to potty train their infants worked. During laboratory experiments early in the twentieth century, scientists discovered that parents were actually teaching their children's muscles to relax and release waste by conditioning the muscles to respond automatically to a parental cue. Squinting when a balloon is about to be popped is an example of this sort of conditioning. In response to the sudden explosion, the muscles of the

Quick Trip

If you think your youngster is purposely misbehaving by refusing to sit on the potty or by wetting and soiling, consider whether you are in some way rewarding him for these problematic behaviors. Some children find negative attention from a parent more rewarding than no attention, so punishing your youngster can backfire and actually encourage the wrong behaviors. Note what your child does right and be sure to point it out.

eye tense, forcing the eyes partially closed. After witnessing several balloons being popped, seeing someone approach another balloon with a long needle is enough to cause the eye muscles to respond by tensing reflexively. At that point, the eye muscles are trained. Such information was used to help parents potty train their children more effectively.

Though this conditioning technique will be covered in detail in later chapters, studies show that you can condition your infant's sphincter muscles by consistently making a special sound when they are open and waste is being released. Once conditioned, you can make the special sound and your child's sphincter muscles will open automatically so that waste is released from the bladder, bowel, or both. As a result, no "trying" on your child's part is involved.

Additional laboratory psychology experiments identified other ways to promote learning. By consistently reinforcing or rewarding certain behaviors and ignoring others, animals and people learn through a procedure called "operant conditioning." The results of this powerful teaching tool have proven truly amazing. Psychologists have gone so far as to teach chickens to play "Twinkle, Twinkle Little Star" on miniature pianos. All a trainer has to do is place a bird in a cage with a small instrument and reward the feathered friend with a food pellet when it accidentally pecks out the first note of the song as it wanders about the cage. If the trainer consistently rewards the bird for pecking out the correct note and ignores all the wrong notes, the fowl soon learns what to do to get a reward. When that happens, it keeps pecking that note. Once it consistently plays the first note, the trainer ups the demands and only rewards the bird when it accidentally pecks out the first two notes of the song in proper sequence. When the bird accidentally succeeds, it is rewarded. Once it consistently succeeds, the trainer increases the demands again and waits to reward the chicken until it accidentally pecks out the first three notes, and so on. Chickens can eventually be trained to play the entire tune.

By using these principles from behavioral psychology, you can speed your child's progress with potty training. The trick is to break the tasks that your youngster needs to learn into a series of small steps. The first step for a young toddler might be sitting on the potty for two seconds, for which she is rewarded. Don't move on to the next step, which might be sitting on the potty for five seconds, until your child has thoroughly mastered the first step and can *consistently* sit on the potty for two seconds when instructed.

Child-Centered Toilet Training

Dr. Benjamin Spock ushered in a new era of more child-friendly parenting with the revolutionary view that youngsters' emotional health and happiness should be considered when deciding how to care for them. He recommended kinder, gentler child-rearing methods and discouraged strict schedules. He suggested that waiting to put babies on the potty until later could make for a happier potty-training experience. He recommended waiting to start potty training until age seven or eight months.

In the 1960s, Dr. Brazelton's potty-training methods came into vogue. He shifted the emphasis from considering children's emotional needs while safeguarding their health to putting their emotional health above all else. He helped convince parents that children could be "clean and dry" by wearing a disposable diaper and urged them not to worry about getting their youngsters potty trained. Brazelton seemed to assume that if children were happy, potty training would take care of itself. Emotional considerations have been the overriding consideration among professionals and parents ever since.

There is no question that children's mental hygiene matters. But physical and emotional health go hand in hand; it is not possible to separate them. Many parents seem to assume that if their children are happy, mental and physical health will follow. They try to make them happy by indulging them. Many parents fulfill their youngsters' desire for snacks throughout the day, their preference for sedentary activities, and their desire to stay up until all hours of the night. Such parenting practices make potty training decidedly more difficult for the following reasons:

- Eating on a schedule helps children develop a pattern of regular elimination. This promotes bowel health and vastly simplifies potty training.
- Daily exercise promotes regularity and lessens problems with constipation. This promotes bowel health and vastly simplifies potty training.
- Sufficient sleep reduces crankiness and irritability. This promotes compliance with parental instructions and vastly simplifies potty training.

The "child-centered approach" involves starting potty training late and adopting a hands-off approach. It is associated with the following physical problems:

- Bladder infections
- Unstable bladder
- Frequent urination
- Bed-wetting

Other problems are associated with delays in potty training:

- Low self-esteem
- Social rejection
- Behavioral problems

In an article published in 2000 titled "Changes in the Toilet Training of Children During the Last Sixty Years: The Cause of an Increase in Lower Urinary Tract Dysfunction?" researchers E. Bakker and J. J. Wyndaele concluded that the answer to their question is yes. They recommend that to avoid permanent bladder dysfunction, parents should start training when children

> **Quick Trip**
>
> Set and enforce limits with your toddler regarding issues such as snacks, bedtime, and playtime to safeguard your child's health and help her learn to follow your instructions. For instance, respond to requests for sugary snacks by offering healthy alternatives, such as vegetable or cheese slices. Practice holding firm until you master the nerve-racking art of letting tantrums run their course. And when a tantrum ends, don't hand your child a cookie! Don't let the fear of another unpleasant scene deter you from holding firm. If your firmness triggers another tantrum or two, so be it. Usually the third time is the charm.

begin to stay dry during the afternoon nap and should use "bladder drill" to teach.

Another large study also provides compelling evidence for a link between late training and long-term toileting problems. Writing in the *Scandinavian Journal of Urology and Nephrology* in 2001, E. Bakker reported the results of a questionnaire evaluating different aspects of personal and familial situations. *All* of the youngsters who had bladder problems at age eleven had started training after age two. Factors that resulted in delayed training included allowing children to proceed at their own pace rather than conducting regular potty sits, letting children sip and snack throughout the day, and dressing them in disposable diapering products rather than cloth.

In actuality, the child-centered approach isn't very child friendly. Parents are human beings and have emotions. When they don't set limits, they are at a loss as to how to get their children to cooperate. Many parents nag to get their child to use the potty, are irritated when their youngster doesn't go, and become upset when the result is an accident. Children learn they have displeased their parent, lose confidence, and feel like failures. But they do not develop self-discipline so they can respond correctly. As a result, the unhappy pattern soon repeats itself. Potty training ends up being stressful for everyone. Stress compromises the immune system and exacts a heavy emotional toll. The indulgent approach doesn't help children learn!

Modern Science

The disposable-diaper industry revolutionized potty training just as formula revolutionized feeding. Companies claimed their scientifically developed products not only equaled Mother Nature but improved upon her. Soon natural methods began to seem antiquated and unhealthy. Breast-feeding has made a minor comeback, but the medical community has yet to question the effect of diapers. Infants in hospitals are swaddled in them, and parents are sent home with a big supply. Parents are not taught that there are better ways to handle elimination.

By eliminating the sensation of wetness, disposables delay the completion of potty training by about a year. They also seem to numb children's bottoms. Toddlers reared in diapers react strongly to the array of unfamiliar sensations when they try to sit on the potty bare bottomed. Some become deeply upset and cannot bear to relieve themselves without wearing a diaper or underwear. Brazelton recommends against removing the diaper too suddenly—to avoid frightening youngsters. Yet most doctors remain convinced that disposable diapering products ease mothers' workloads, keep babies clean, and are necessary for maintaining a sanitary environment. Nothing indicates that any of these are true.

A review of research reported in the official scientific journal of the American Academy of Pediatrics, *Pediatrics*, turns up a number of startling findings. Experts have established that infants possess the physical capability to delay elimination and respond to cues to use a potty as early as two or three months. Max Maizels, professor of urology at Northwestern University's medical school and the attending urologist at Children's Memorial Hospital in Chicago, stated in a 1993 article in *Current Problems in Pediatrics* that by the end of infancy, children can sense bladder fullness and have the muscle skills necessary to postpone urinating. Timothy Schum's research led him to conclude that children with a mental age of twenty-one months are ready to *finish* training. By then, most toddlers can remove their clothes and handle the mechanics of the potty by themselves. For your child to have a chance to finish by then, you need to start working with him well in advance.

Most authors of potty-training books and articles lead readers to believe that children under age two lack the physical capability to postpone elimination. Author Jan Faull goes so far as to inform readers that babies "leak." Faull suggests that grandparents who say their young toddler was potty trained are exaggerating or have faulty memories, despite the fact that parents have been training infants, babies, and young toddlers since the dawn of humankind.

Modern scientists subtly discourage parents from training in other ways. Today, the American Academy of Pediatrics' toilet-training guidelines state, "Bowel and bladder control is a necessary *social skill*." [Italics added.] This suggests that being potty trained is required for sound interpersonal relationships. While developing control of elimination is a definite boon to popularity, that is *not* why achieving continence is important!

- Toilet training is necessary for personal hygiene and cleanliness.
- Toilet training protects bladder health.
- Toilet training protects against infection.

- Developmentally, toileting is an essential *self-care* skill—a critical step on the long road to growing up and becoming independent.

Few U.S. pediatricians even seem to have heard of infant potty training. When they are informed about it, many deny its possibility based on their understanding of children's physical limitations. Learning what is involved and seeing an infant in action should convince these pediatricians that their professors in medical school misinformed them about children's physical capabilities. Yet, many physicians persist in the opinion that infant training is impossible and should not be attempted. They need to educate themselves on the subject.

In the meantime, you need to decide what is in your child's best physical and emotional interest. Every child and every family situation are different. But before deciding how and when to begin, educate yourself as to the pros and cons of giving your child an early start. To do that, keep reading.

Question and Answer

My husband occasionally leaves the bathroom door open when relieving himself. Should I be concerned that my two-and-a-half-year-old son sees his father using the toilet?

Quite the contrary. It is best that your son not be made to feel there is anything shameful about using the bathroom. In fact, allowing him to see that this is a normal activity will help with potty training. In a year or two, seeing other family members without clothes on may make your child uncomfortable. If he requests that the bathroom door remain closed, respect his wishes.

3

Potty-Training Travel Guide

Before Your Departure

Amanda dreaded having to potty train her daughter. In truth, the very word training *made her uncomfortable. It brought to mind an image of housebreaking a puppy by swatting it with a rolled-up newspaper or of training a dolphin by doling out bites of fish as rewards. Her daughter was generally easygoing and cooperative, yet it was hard to think of anything her eighteen-month-old was actually "trained" to do. Of late she had resisted when Amanda tried to buckle her into her car seat, never mind that her mother had been 100 percent consistent about putting on her seat belt.*

When Amanda asked her daughter's pediatrician about potty training, he responded by talking about "potty learning." Amanda supposed that meant she was to serve as her daughter's teacher, which definitely sounded better than being her trainer. But when she pondered the matter later, she wondered exactly what that meant. Was she supposed to put together lesson plans, assign homework, and administer tests? Once again, her confidence waned.

Amanda visited her sister in hopes of picking up some pointers. As they chatted in the kitchen, Amanda's seven-month-old niece suddenly turned toward her potty, waved a little fist, and gurgled. "Yes! Potty!" her mother exclaimed. She made a sort of a fist and twisted her hand back and forth. "That's sign language," she explained. Amanda watched in amazement as her sister quickly unsnapped her daughter's romper, carried her to the potty, and then smiled and clapped as the baby used it.

"Wow!" Amanda enthused. "You're a great potty teacher!"

Her sister frowned and shook her head. "It's called elimination communication, or EC for short," her sister said firmly. "It's not like I'm an expert stuffing knowledge in her head. It's a partnership. We guide each other, figuring things out as we go along."

Despite her sister's reproving tone, Amanda liked the idea that she and her daughter would be working together. For the first time, Amanda felt equal to the task.

Many professionals have sought to clarify what is involved in acquiring toileting skills by talking about *potty learning* instead of *potty training*. Because some animal trainers force obedience by punishing their charges and fitness trainers put flab-fighting students through grueling workouts, the term *potty training* can give parents the wrong impression about their role and how to proceed. Most people assume that sitting on a potty is required to learn to use it, so potty training an infant sounds cruel. They expect a potty-trained child to handle all aspects of toileting without help, so the idea of training youngsters too young to walk to the potty by themselves, manage clothing, and clean themselves up afterward makes no sense. The terms people use can limit their thinking.

Some professionals and parents dislike the term *infant potty training*, preferring *elimination communication* (EC) or *natural infant hygiene* instead. The former reflects the emphasis on communication—learning to recognize and respond to the signals infants give when they need to pee and poop. The latter reflects the emphasis on using natural methods to keep them clean and dry while helping them exercise their muscles and stay connected to their bodies. Infants do gain a lot of experience eliminating into a little potty, and the results are often impressive. Many six-month-olds who have been worked with from birth rarely wet the bed or have accidents. Nevertheless, parents commonly end up viewing their infant's concrete potty accomplishments as relatively insignificant compared to the other benefits. The real miracle, they say, is the intimacy that develops. From working with their infant so intensively, they get to know one another at a deeper level, develop a closer connection, and become more bonded. Hence, many believe the term *infant potty training* fails to capture the essence and power of what transpires.

Nevertheless, this book uses the term *potty training* for all the steps toward enabling the children to tend to toileting by themselves. It includes everything from observing your infant without a diaper to helping your young toddler undress for potty practices to teaching your elementary-school student how to change the sheets after a bout of bed-wetting. Whatever term you use, your role will in many ways be like that of a tour guide. You must make

Quick Trip

The term *potty training* may seem more appealing if setting limits comes naturally to you. If you find it easier to empathize and respond to your child's feelings, you may be drawn to the term *potty learning*. Whichever term you use, toddlers and older children are likely to need both limits and empathy to master the potty. To become more adept at setting limits, choose a small issue and practice holding firm. To become more responsive to your child's feelings, pause to listen and communicate that you understand. If your youngster is upset, provide some time for venting before you set limits.

the arrangements, handle the details, gather and communicate information, and strive to make your youngster's journey pleasant.

Travel Dictionaries

Your first task before heading out on your potty-training expedition is to choose a set of vocabulary words and phrases. Your second task is to stick with them. Repetition is the name of the game when learning a foreign language. Babies and toddlers have only recently arrived on the planet, so their comprehension of English remains poor. Changing the words and phrases you use to describe the potty and elimination muddies the verbal waters and causes confusion.

To get the idea of what tots are up against when they try to make sense of explanations and instructions, consider the plight for adult foreign-language students. Learning that the French expression "*Ça va?*" means "How are you?" doesn't help them comprehend "*Comment allez-vous?*" and "*Est-que vous allez bien?*" which carry the same meaning. Similarly, just because a youngster understands "Go to the potty," doesn't mean that she also understands "It's time to use the toilet " or "You'd better head on into the bathroom." Research shows that babies and toddlers comprehend *less* than their parents think. For little ones, English is still a foreign language.

Potty-Training Vocabulary

It is best to use the correct terms or their popular kiddy counterparts and avoid heavy slang. You may think it is cute when your two-year-old proudly announces, "Me piss in john!" But pediatricians find such language off-putting, teachers view it as rude, and other parents may be so offended that they will cancel your child's play dates.

Technical Terms	Popular Words
Urine	Pee, pee-pee, wee-wee
Bowel movement	Poop
Feces	Poo-poo
Stool	BM, number 2
To void	To pee
To urinate	Make pee-pee, go wee-wee
To defecate	Poop
To pass stool	Go poo-poo
To have a bowel movement	Do number 2
To have a BM	Poo
Use the toilet	Go potty
Eliminate, pass waste	Wet or soil
Buttocks	Butt, bottom, bum, tush

Technical Vocabulary

Being familiar with the technical vocabulary can help you understand the finer points of elimination. This can come in handy when communicating with doctors about special problems.

Term	Definition
Anal and bladder sphincters	Muscles that control the release of waste
Anus	Opening through which solid waste passes from the body
Bladder	Organ that stores urine
Buttocks	Flesh surrounding the anus
Constipation	Hard, painful bowel movements
Continent	Able to avoid accidental wetting and soiling

Detrusor muscles	Bowel and bladder muscles that contract to expel waste
Diarrhea	Frequent passage of watery stool
Eliminate	Expel urine or stool from the body
Encopresis/fecal incontinence	Uncontrolled soiling
Enuresis	Uncontrolled wetting
Incomplete voiding	Some urine remains in the bladder after urinating
Incontinent	Unable to avoid wetting and soiling
Kidney	Organ that filters the blood and excretes waste as urine
Large intestine	Part of the bowel that forms and moves solid waste toward the rectum
Meconium	Substance expelled from the bowel after birth
Nocturnal enuresis	Chronic bed-wetting
	Primary: has never been consistently dry at night
	Secondary: resumed bed-wetting after staying dry for a month
Pelvic floor muscles	Muscles that open and close the urethra and anal canals to contain and release waste
Rectum	Lower portion of the bowel that stores solid waste
Urethra	Tube that conducts urine from the bladder toward the outside of the body

Quick Trip

Shorter phrases are easier for babies and toddlers to comprehend than long sentences. Instead of saying, "It's time to go to the potty now" or even "Go to the potty now," stick to "Go potty" until your child's language skills are well developed.

Urethral opening/meatus	Opening through which urine leaves the body
	Boys: located at the tip of the penis
	Girls: located between the vaginal opening and clitoris
Urge to urinate or defecate	Bladder or bowel is contracting to expel waste
UTI	Urinary tract infection

A Journey Inside

The process of elimination is actually very simple.

• **Step 1: Liquid waste flows into the bladder and solid waste into the bowel.** Because of their small organs and frequent feedings, infants pass waste frequently. Elimination becomes less frequent as children grow, and the stool becomes harder and more formed.

• **Step 2: Pressure inside the bladder and bowel increases.** The rising pressure as waste accumulates creates the physical sensation of needing to urinate or have a bowel movement.

• **Step 3: The brain signals the bladder or bowel to expel waste.** When the pressure inside these organs becomes too

Quick Trip

Intense emotion can cause the bladder to contract suddenly and expel urine. Hence the expressions, "I was so scared, I wet my pants" and "I laughed so hard, I wet my pants." Similarly, a sudden change in pressure caused by a cough or giggle can sometimes start bladder contractions. If your child is sitting on the potty with a full bladder but can't relax enough to use it, some gentle tickles may produce some trickles.

intense, a series of muscular contractions begins to expel waste. They create the sudden urge to urinate or have a bowel movement. The contractions are similar to those of the uterus that expel a baby during labor.

• **Step 4: The sphincter muscles open and allow waste to flow from the body.** The sphincter muscles, which encircle the bowel and bladder openings like nooses, are normally drawn tight to keep waste from escaping. To release waste, the sphincters must be relaxed. To relax the sphincters, the pelvic floor muscles must be lowered. When children are told to push to try to use the potty, they may raise the pelvic floor muscles instead. The result is that the sphincters remain closed and prevent waste from being released.

Most of the time the sphincter muscles remain closed to keep waste inside the body. There are three ways for the sphincters to open so that waste can be released.

1. Before potty training, the sphincters operate by reflex, opening and closing on their own.
2. During infant and baby training, parents condition their youngster's sphincter muscles to open on cue.

3. During baby and toddler training, children learn to relax their sphincters to release waste voluntarily before the pressure triggers a reflex that opens them and causes an accident.

Mapping the Journey

In his book published by the British Psychological Association, author Herbert Martin noted that the typical progression toward being fully potty trained is as follows:

1. Daytime bowel control
2. Nighttime bowel control
3. Daytime bladder control
4. Nighttime bladder control

Bowel control probably comes first because children often pass gas, grunt, or strain before and during bowel movements, making it easier for parents to recognize what is happening, point it out, and get their youngsters to the potty in time to use it. The bladder sphincter also opens when children poop, so pee is released as well. While learning to use the potty for bowel movements, many children learn to pee in it at the same time.

The fact that many children have a bowel movement at about the same time each day would also seem to speed learning, since their parents can get them to the potty at the right time consistently. However, regularity may not be as much of an advantage as professionals have thought. In an investigation of toilet training conducted by researcher Timothy R. Schum, children who were less regular actually made faster progress with bowel training than more regular ones.

It is impossible to predict the order of learning for a given child or how fast she will learn. Research suggests that less adaptable children are harder to work with and take longer to learn than youngsters who are less upset by change. However, other aspects of temperament that would seem important don't predict how long children will take to finish potty training. Parents are often surprised that their hyperactive hellion learns quickly while their compliant perfectionist has great difficulty. Worries about performing and pleasing can make conscientious rule-followers too physically tense to release waste, resulting in slower progress. Perhaps overly active children are more amenable to dropping what they are doing to head off for the potty. It could be that because their parents anticipate problems, they are more careful to avoid power struggles. The only identifiable pattern is that children tend to finish training in the time frame generally considered proper in their culture, which can range from age six months to three years.

Some factors are known to slow progress for individual children. A potty-training trauma can cause potty resistance and refusals, creating a setback. For instance, a sudden fright from a loud noise while being held over a potty may prove terribly upsetting to an infant. A hard fall off a potty can cause a baby to become hysterical the next time he's placed on it. An unexpected splash of cold water when hard stool lands in the toilet bowl can frighten young toddlers. Because even preschool children can't distinguish between fantasy and reality very well, a scary dream about the potty can cause them to avoid it.

A common cause of slow potty-training progress is constipation. More than half of older toddlers suffer occasional or ongoing problems with hard movements that are painful to pass. Many youngsters associate the pain with the potty and avoid pooping in it. They may have continuing difficulties with bowel training long after they stop wetting. Others avoid the potty altogether and training stalls for a time. Don't assume that your resistant tot is just being contrary! Putting away the potty and giving your child time to forget the trauma before resuming practice sessions may mean faster progress overall.

It is not possible to predict how your youngster will fair with staying dry at night. About 3 percent of twelve-month-olds stay dry without undergoing any type of training, according to toilet-training researcher Akihiro Kawauchi. Although many toddlers begin spontaneously awakening dry in the mornings, the more common pattern is for young children to stop wetting the bed soon after they have made enough progress with potty training to stay dry during the day. Kawauchi found that when parents waited to begin potty training until the late toddler years, their youngsters took about fourteen months to achieve nighttime dryness. As many as 20 percent continued to wet the bed until age five, and hefty percentages continued throughout elementary school.

Certain physical problems can cause elimination difficulties. For instance, weak pelvic floor muscles can make it hard or impossible for children to contain urine or stool so they can avoid wetting and soiling. They may be unable to push so they can empty the bladder completely, causing them to urinate frequently. Chronically tense pelvic floor muscles can make urinating and passing bowel movements difficult and may cause pain. A urine stream that is very weak or inconsistent rather than steady can be a sign of improper functioning of the pelvic floor muscles due to trauma, infection, or congenital malformations. Excessive straining during elimination and postponing elimination for long periods can injure the muscles. Because the central nervous system coordinates the action of the pelvic muscles with that of the bladder and bowel, neurological disorders can also cause elimination problems. Sexual abuse can damage the pelvic floor muscles and upset the functioning of the central nervous system. Sexual abuse is a risk factor for chronic toileting problems and bed-wetting; an estimated 25 percent of sexually abused children wet the bed. Other conditions that cause bed-wetting are described in Chapter 10, and several bowel problems are discussed in Appendix A.

Quick Trip

Constipation is more common among children after age two but can occur at any age. Because painful bowel movements are known to cause potty refusals and withholding of stool (known as *psychological constipation*), check regularly during potty training to make sure the movements are soft. A number of causes and treatments for constipation are discussed in Appendix A. If constipation persists, discuss the matter with your health-care provider.

Speeding Communication

To jump-start your child's ability to communicate and to make potty training easier, teach her a bit of sign language. Babies gain control of their fingers and hands before their vocal chords, tongue, and lips. Children don't begin to speak until about twelve months, while youngsters reared by deaf parents begin signing about four months earlier, at an average age of eight months. If worked with from birth, some six-month-olds begin making rudimentary signs that their parents can decipher. By learning to sign, they can express their need for diaper changes and the potty sooner.

Teaching your child to sign is easy. Communicating through gestures comes naturally to babies. They pull away from the nipple when they have had enough to eat, yawn when they are sleepy, and avert their eyes when they are ready for playtime to end. Teaching babies to sign is surprisingly simple. They learn by repeatedly seeing a specific gesture and hearing it paired with a spoken word or being shown its meaning. Whenever you say the word *diaper*, give the sign at the same time or point to a diaper. The challenge is to train *yourself* to make the sign every time you say the word.

Here are some baby signs that can help you and your child communicate during potty training:

Diaper: (Used by babies when they need a diaper change. Used by parents to ask whether the diaper needs to be changed and to indicate that it is time to change the diaper.) Pat the back of the upper thigh.

Dirty: (Used by children to indicate that it is time for them to be changed.) Wiggle the fingers of the right hand under the chin, with the palm facing down.

Good: (Used by parents as praise or approval and by children to express pride or pleasure in an accomplishment.) Raise one or both thumbs in the thumbs-up sign.

Help: (Used for "I need help," "Can I help you?" and "Let me help you.") Place the fist of one hand on the palm of the other hand, and raise your arms so both hands slide upward at the same time.

Hurry: (Used for "Hurry up" and "I'm in a hurry.") Place the arms at the sides, palms facing the thighs, and extend the index and middle fingers of each hand. Repeatedly bend and straighten the elbows so that the hands arc up and down from the level of the thighs to the head. Alternate the hands so that when one is moving up, the other is moving down.

Potty: (Used for both "I need to go potty" and "Do you need to go potty?") Make the sign for the letter *T* in American Sign Language (the letter *T* doubles as the sign for *toilet*) by placing the thumb between the index and middle finger, then twist the wrist so the hand moves back and forth. Babies tend to wave their fist up and down rather than rotating it from side to side.

Wash: (Used for *wash, clean,* and *wipe,* as in "We need to wash your hands," "I need to clean up this puddle," or "Let Mommy wipe your bottom.") Place your palms together, with one palm facing up and the other facing down. With the top hand, make a circular motion as though polishing something.

Wrong: (Used to gently admonish a child or to let her know she has done something incorrectly.) Make a Y by extending the thumb and pinky finger of the right hand and folding down the middle three fingers. With the palm facing the body, raise the hand to the chin.

Though there are several good books on baby signing, it's easier to learn signs by watching a video than by looking at still pictures in a book. The quality of the videos varies, so read the reviews before buying. A popular DVD or video, *Baby See 'n Sign*, was selected as one of *Parenting* magazine's best 2002 videos.

Avid baby signers have shown that they have lots more on their minds than adults ever imagined. It's not surprising that once little ones can communicate their wants and needs, they have fewer frustration-driven tantrums. Parents note that they are less frustrated once they can get their messages across. The improvements in overall mood and behavior as well as the enhanced communication make signing a good bet for speeding and easing potty training.

Question and Answer

Can't I just make up gestures for communicating with my baby instead of learning the proper signs?

It is possible for you and your baby to invent gestures. But since many day-care workers know a bit of American Sign Language, it is better to teach the standard signs and supplement them with your family's creations. Be sure to teach the signs to sitters and other caregivers so your tot can communicate her needs to others.

4

Parents' Trip Kit

Packing for Your Journey

At his first birthday party, Jerrod was more interested in playing with the ribbons than in opening his presents, so his mother did the honors for him. The gift from their next-door neighbor was a little outfit.

"It's darling!" Chantal exclaimed. But when she held it up for the other mothers to admire, she noticed a large hole in the pants. It started at the crotch and ran halfway up the back.

"It's supposed to be that way. It's a potty-training outfit," her neighbor said. "I bought it in China. See? The fabric has been stitched to keep it from fraying. Chinese toddlers don't wear anything underneath. When they sit down on their potty, the fabric gapes open. When they're outside, they just squat to do their business."

The other adults exchanged glances. "That's yucky," an eight-year-old guest exclaimed, expressing everyone's opinion.

"I was kind of shocked at first," the neighbor said. "But Chinese moms thought it sounded worse to let babies use their diapers as toilets. Besides, they thought all that changing and all that laundry would be too much work."

Chantal smiled. "They've got it right about the laundry!" She paused, then shook her head. "Going to the bathroom in the street seems so—so unsanitary."

"I know. But that same mess is about to be on Jerrod's little bum." Sure enough, Jerrod's face was red. He was obviously straining. Chantal sighed. She was so sick of changing him. One year down and what—another year, maybe two still to go?

"Most moms in our country want their kids out of diapers for their own convenience," her neighbor said. Chantal blushed, wondering if her neighbor had read her mind. "But that seems selfish, so we put off potty training, thinking we're doing our kids a favor," her neighbor continued. "In China, I realized that potty training is really about hygiene. We're not helping our kids by keeping them in diapers longer than absolutely necessary."

It hadn't occurred to Chantal that being potty trained was in Jerrod's best interest. Now that she thought about it, she could see that it was. And if she reaped some benefits, so much the better.

There are several approaches to managing children's pee and poop: catching it in a little pot, catching it in disposable diapers, catching it in cloth diapers, or a combination of the three. Using a pot and forgoing diapers altogether is very taxing. Even parents who do infant potty training usually dress their child in diapers some of the time. Disposable diapers are not a good choice for potty training because they eliminate the sensation of wetness, which slows learning. Before stocking up on disposables, it is important to consider the merits of cloth diapers.

Elimination is a natural part of the digestive process. However, there is nothing natural about containing waste in diapers where it is smeared across children's bottoms and ground into their genitals and pores. When waste is held close to the body in a warm, moist environment, bacteria flourish. Urine, which contains ammonia, burns the skin. Prolonged contact causes *necrosis* (tissue death) and can leave permanent scars. Although ammonia burns have been given the benign name of "diaper rash," there is nothing benign about burning a baby's skin with ammonia! Besides being painful, the sores are breeding grounds for viral, bacterial, and fungal infections.

Poop contains *E. coli* bacteria. Amounts too small to be seen with the naked eye can enter the bloodstream via the mouth, eye, or a cut on the skin. *E. coli* gives off a toxic chemical that produces severe abdominal pain, cramping, and watery diarrhea. This toxin also damages the blood vessels, so the diarrhea becomes bloody as the bacteria multiply. Usually the immune system destroys the infection in five to ten days. But for children under five, the loss of fluid and blood can create serious medical problems. According to the U.S. Food and Drug Administration (FDA), approximately 5 to 10 percent of children who become ill from *E. coli* progress to hemolytic uremic syndrome, which can cause permanent kidney damage. According to the website of the Centers for Disease Control and Prevention, "toddlers who are not toilet trained, as well as their family members and playmates, are at high risk of becoming infected."

Infant's waste is sanitary. In fact, most mammal moms clean up after their young by consuming it. As their offspring mature, their waste becomes a health hazard. At that point babies are taught to pee and poop outside the family nest, away from where the family eats and sleeps. Soon after kittens open their eyes, they are taught how to dig a small hole and bury their waste in the family litter box or in a soft patch of ground.

The most baby-friendly technique is to catch your child's waste in a small pot starting at birth. By learning how to do this before the waste develops a strong odor and becomes a health hazard, your misses won't be such a problem. Still, parents may at times dress their infants in diapers during the day, and many

Quick Trip

Putting the word *natural* on product labels boosts sales to parents who are concerned about protecting the earth's most vulnerable human inhabitants: infants and babies. But products may nevertheless contain dangerous chemicals. Find out what is in creams, ointments, wipes, powders, and oils before applying them to your baby's delicate skin. The skin is the largest organ, and some chemicals can irritate it. Others can be absorbed into the body. Avoid perfumed products, including scented disposable diapers and wipes. When buying clothes, look for natural fabrics, such as unbleached cotton. Continuous exposure to strong chemicals, individually or in combination, can trigger adverse reactions from toxic overload—tomorrow if not today.

rely on them at night. If having your child go diaperless is not a possibility, choose diapers conducive to potty training and start working toward the goal of getting your youngster trained as soon as possible.

Slings and Things

It is unlikely that Mother Nature intended for young humans to have their bottoms covered most every moment of every day and night and to spend most of their time lying on beds or in rigid carriers. Indigenous mothers from many cultures carry their naked babies in slings. That way, they can detect the small movements and faint sounds that signal their youngster's need to eliminate and quickly extricate her to avoid accidents.

Slings may provide some other important potty-training benefits. The continuous swaying motion provides a long, gentle massage for the baby's bottom. Because problems with colic and constipation often clear up after parents begin using a sling, author Ingrid Bauer conjectures that the movement may be beneficial. In *Infant Potty Training*, author Laurie Boucke notes that other mammal parents stimulate digestion and elimination by licking their young. She believes that slings may provide important physical stimulation for human babies.

The constant physical contact between mother and child provided by a sling may facilitate bonding and strengthen attachment, thereby reducing potty-training conflicts down the road. Riding in a sling ends the long, dreary hours of isolation and immobility that are unhappy realities for babies left in cribs, playpens, plastic carriers, and strollers. A happier youngster is likely to be more cooperative and have more energy to devote to potty training.

Mexican *rebozos* and Guatemalan wraps are popular slings used by many American moms engaged in infant potty training. Brands such as the SlingEZee, Maya Wrap, and Over the Shoulder Baby Holders are available in a variety of delightful colors and fabrics from nurturedfamily.com. Safety tips and advice for using slings, including details for putting them on to ensure the health

Quick Trip

It is best to choose a traditional sling rather than a baby carrier styled like a backpack. Even though carriers can also be worn on the chest, getting children in and out of them is awkward. The time between an infant's signal and the start of elimination is short, so time is of the essence.

and comfort of both mother and baby, can be viewed at char lottescloset.com.

Diapering Decisions

There are a number of compelling reasons to avoid disposable diapering products. To potty train your child, he needs to be able to feel the wetness so he can come to recognize the sensation, associate it with the act of passing waste, and eventually learn to identify the sensation of needing to eliminate in advance. Moreover, disposable diapers and pull-up training pants are not minor players in the decimation of the earth's resources. In fact, they are huge contributors.

Air-pollution experts have issued warnings about dioxin, a toxic by-product of the paper manufacturing process. City managers across the country are struggling to cope with the forty-five million diapers containing raw, untreated waste added to U.S. landfills each year. Although the government has declined to pass laws outlawing the release of dangerous pollutants into the air and water, more parents are expressing a willingness to sacrifice to help ensure that the Earth remains habitable for the next generation. Fortunately, forgoing disposables is likely to turn out to be less of a sacrifice than you might think.

In an era when time is more valuable than money, ads suggesting that disposable products save time convince families of their value. But are disposable diapers actually time-savers? Assuming ten or eleven diaper changes per day for a newborn, seven or eight daily changes from then until age two, and five or six daily changes thereafter, the average child requires 6,500 disposable diapers and pull-up training pants from birth to age two and a half. Children reared in disposables require an extra year, on average, to complete potty training, so cloth diapers can eliminate the need for several thousand diaper changes!

And you won't have to spend so much time working to earn the money to pay for cloth diapers, either. The cost of a disposable diaper ranges between $0.30 and $0.95. After two and a half years, the total comes to about $2,000 for inexpensive brands and $6,000 for premium products. The cost of a diaper service runs about $0.25 per diaper, which totals approximately $1,625 for two and a half years. The price includes diapers, pickup, and delivery. You don't even have to rinse wet diapers or scrape poopy ones before returning them to the company. Industrial washing machines use a dozen wash and rinse cycles to ensure that diapers are properly sanitized and that the correct pH is attained to help prevent diaper rash.

If you would rather save money than time, you can buy cloth diapers and launder them at home. Cheap cotton brands sell for less than $1.00 each, but they may not last the distance. Top-of-

Quick Trip

Some disposable diapers feature pictures that fade when the diaper is wet. This makes it easier for parents to see when a diaper change is needed, but the benefits for children remain questionable. Some parents report their youngsters' motivation to stay dry improved after being told not to wet so as not to ruin the pictures. Other parents say that moisture still wicks away from the skin before their children could detect it, preventing them from comprehending the process of elimination. They couldn't figure out how to keep the pictures from dissolving.

the-line, European unbleached cotton diapers sell for $2.75 each and can be handed down to a younger sibling. To get started, you will need about two dozen, bringing the cost to about $66. Cleaning agents, energy, and water cost about $600 to $850 for two and a half years. You will also need to purchase diaper wraps, covers, and liners (described later), which can add several hundred dollars more to the total. That's still just a fraction of what you would pay for disposables.

Cloth Diapering Systems

If you remember tots from generations past trudging about with droopy, drippy cloth britches or wearing thick rubber or stiff plastic pants to prevent problematic puddles, rest assured that those days are long gone. In the last fifty years, cloth diapering has undergone a dramatic transformation, and the problems that disposables were designed to solve have been all but eliminated. Today's multilayered cloth diapering system makes for tidier youngsters and less harried parents by reducing bulk, deterring leaks, and by simplifying cleanup. A wide range of fabrics and styles is available. For instance, organic cotton is free of the dyes and chemicals to which some babies react, and new synthetic materials wick wetness away from the skin. There are even diapers and diaper covers with navel cutouts for newborns. The heart of the system is still a cloth diaper, but it has been completely refashioned.

Cloth Diapers

Good-quality cloth diapers now provide superabsorbency via as many as six layers of cotton. There are several ways to achieve a good fit without the complex folding techniques used by past generations of parents. For instance, fitted diapers are available. They are expensive, but because children typically outgrow them before they wear out, it is often possible to pick them up at thrift stores and garage sales for just pennies on the dollar.

Most parents and diaper services use prefold diapers. Prefolds are much smaller than traditional flat diapers. They come in several sizes so no complicated folding is required. Infants don't end up encased in a big, bulky fabric while toddlers appear to be bulging at the seams. Once outgrown, smaller diapers can be folded in thirds and placed inside larger diapers for additional protection. Prefolds feature extra padding in the center where more absorbency is needed and thinner edges for a comfier fit. Some prefolds have polyester strips sewn onto the edges to prevent fraying. Rectangular prefolds are used by diaper services and most parents. However, some parents prefer contoured prefolds. They are shaped like an hourglass to reduce the bulk between the legs.

Diapering Techniques

The art to cloth diapering involves making sure the fit is snug at the waist and leg openings. The diaper must be tight enough to prevent leaks without being so tight as to leave red marks. For closing flat and prefold diapers, traditional metal safety pins have been redesigned. They are curved rather than straight to lessen the likelihood of sticking the baby or yourself. Instead of safety pins, a plastic device called a Snappi can be used. Its teeth grip the diaper on each side.

Fitted diapers typically close with snaps or elastic. The problem with snaps is that diapers in many different sizes may be needed to get a proper fit as a baby grows, while elastic may not withstand the chemicals required for proper laundering. The most popular diapering technique is to use a prefold diaper and

cover it with a breathable diaper wrap. The wrap holds the diaper in place and helps contain wetness. Wraps with Velcro closures are ideal for potty training because they can be removed
quickly.

Diaper Covers

The diaper wraps used to hold prefold diapers in place help contain wetness. However, a wrap can still get wet if your child urinates heavily. Past generations of parents used rubber or plastic
pants. The modern version—diaper covers—are made in a variety of soft fabrics that breathe to prevent heat buildup. Nylon
covers are lightweight, making them desirable on hot days. Fleece
covers are good choices for heavy wetters and for additional
warmth in winter. Microfiber fabrics, which are used to make
sports garments, help wick moisture away from the baby's skin,
making them a popular choice for use at night.

Wool covers are considered the Rolls-Royce of the diaper
world. Good quality, untreated wool is soft rather than scratchy,
is cool in summer and warm in winter, and can be machine
washed and line dried. Although wool can hold up to a third of
its weight in liquid before it feels damp, it breathes to prevent
heat buildup.

All-in-one diapers have a diaper cover sewn to the outside of
a fitted diaper. They are convenient but may be difficult to launder. The covers cannot usually withstand all of the heavy-duty
washing required to sanitize the diaper.

Diaper Liners

Diaper liners fit inside cloth diapers. Liners are so popular that
some fitted diapers have a pocket sewn inside to hold liners in
place. During the first few days of life, liners protect cloth diapers from being permanently stained by meconium, which is dis-

charged from a newborn's bowels. Thereafter, disposable and flushable paper liners eliminate the chore of scraping poopy diapers.

Economy flannelette diaper liners can be used once and tossed out, if your budget permits. Otherwise, they can be laundered and reused. It is possible to make your own cloth liners by cutting strips of fabric purchased from a yard goods store or by ripping up flannel or cotton sheets from a thrift store. You don't even need to hem them if you use them only once before discarding. Put soiled liners in a plastic bag and place in the trash as you would a disposable diaper.

Other popular reusable liners are made of polyester mesh or polar fleece, which wick moisture from the baby's skin to help prevent diaper rash. They are good choices for nighttime use. Poop does not readily stick to these synthetic fabrics, so it can usually be shaken off the liner into the toilet. Poopy cotton liners may need to be scraped into the toilet but have other advantages. They are absorbent, and some are large enough to serve as diapers for newborns. Later they can be placed inside a regular diaper for extra absorbency at night.

Laundering Diapers

Before putting cloth diapers on your child, wash them two to three times to remove the coating and fluff the fibers so they can reach maximum absorbency. Be aware that cotton diapers will shrink. Avoid fabric softeners and detergents that are advertised as being especially gentle, such as Ivory, or that are supposed to be environmentally friendly. Such products coat the cotton fibers, which reduces absorbency.

Dirty diapers can be stored in a plastic bag closed with a twist tie when you are out and about. At home, keep dirty diapers in a covered diaper pail until they are ready to be washed. Start removing stains and sanitizing them by storing them in a pail filled with cold water and a half cup of borax. (Hot water sets stains.) After your baby starts eating solid foods, you will need to scrape poopy diapers into the toilet and keep them in a separate pail.

You may want to run diapers that have been soaking in a pail through the spin cycle on your washer to remove excess water before laundering. Poopy diapers should be machine washed three times. The first time, use a half cup of Arm and Hammer washing soda, laundry detergent, and cold water. The second time, add the wet diapers to the washer with another half cup of washing soda, more laundry detergent, and warm water. Then put the same load through a third wash using another half cup of washing soda with laundry detergent and hot water. Add an extra rinse cycle to remove soap residue. If the diapers don't smell clean, run them through a fourth wash cycle, with more washing soda and detergent.

Washing soda adds cleaning power and helps get the correct pH to help prevent diaper rash. Alternatively, nonchlorine bleach, borax, or both can be used to brighten and whiten diapers. Avoid chlorine bleach, which is hard on the fabric. Adding

Quick Trip

Unless they get wet, diaper wraps and covers can be worn more than once before needing to be laundered. Follow the instructions for washing and drying carefully so as not to ruin the fabric. Rather than putting them in the dryer, you may need to lay them out to air dry. Close Velcro tabs before laundering to keep them from picking up lint and mangling other garments. If Velcro becomes linty, run a comb through the loops to clean them.

white vinegar to the final rinse also helps remove soap residue and get the proper pH. To remove stubborn stains, line dry the diapers in the sun for several hours. The ultraviolet rays are a natural disinfectant.

Follow the instructions carefully for washing and drying diaper covers and wraps so as not to ruin the fabrics. Rather than putting them in the dryer, you may need to lay them out to air dry. Velcro tabs need to be closed before laundering to keep them from picking up lint and mangling other garments. If Velcro becomes linty, run a comb through the loops to clean them.

Potty-Training Wardrobes

When potty training toddlers, the popular practice is to dress them in disposable training pants. They pull up and down like underwear, so toddlers can get them on and off easily. Training pants provide the excitement and ego boost of being a "big kid." Unfortunately, disposable training pants also eliminate the sensation of wetness. Children have a tendency to forget they are wearing them and may continue wetting and soiling as if they were wearing a regular disposable diaper. Cloth training pants are styled like underwear but have additional padding at the crotch. They help reduce the mess of accidents without eliminating the sensation of wetness. For more reliable protection, add a diaper cover.

Getting to wear underpants can be a big incentive for toddlers to stay dry once they have learned to use the potty. Consider letting your youngster help choose which kind to buy. To increase his motivation to use the potty, you might make a rule that he can only wear his big-kid underpants as long as he can keep them dry. If he has an accident, redress him in training pants or diapers. Explain that if he uses the potty while wearing training pants or diapers, he can put on his underpants again.

Quick Trip

Work on teaching your untrained toddler how to get his pants down whenever you are undressing him. Show him how to tuck a thumb inside the waistband and pull the fabric out as well as down so the pants slide past the diaper.

For outerwear, Chinese baby and toddler pants and rompers are especially desirable because the pants are open at the crotch. They are meant to be worn without anything underneath so that children don't have to take them off to use the potty. This type of clothing is not easy to find in stores, but it can be purchased online at charlottescloset.com. Hand sewn by work-at-home moms and priced between ten and fifteen dollars each, the company offers two styles. The traditional split pants are like the ones Chinese toddlers wear. The conservative pants, which are especially popular with U.S. parents, look like more like regular pants. Fabric choices include fleece for cooler months and cotton or a polyester blend for summer.

Otherwise, choose clothing your child can remove quickly:

- Avoid clothes with small buttons and complicated closures.
- Choose loose-fitting pants with elastic waistbands or Velcro closures for boys.
- Dress girls in skirts and dresses.

Pint-Sized Potties

Any type of receptacle can be used for infant waste. Because you will be holding your child in your arms while she eliminates, a bathtub, laundry tub, toilet, pot, pan, or small mixing bowl will suffice. The only requirement is that the receptacle should be slightly larger than your baby's bottom. One infant potty-training technique to be discussed later involves resting your baby on your lap during feedings while holding a bowl between your thighs. To do this, you will need a bowl that is small enough so your baby cannot fall in if you relax your grip or shift positions.

The upper lip of the bowl should be rounded so it doesn't cut into your baby's bottom. Glass containers are less than ideal because they may break if dropped; soft plastic bowls have the disadvantage of staining and retaining odors. Consider metal, hard plastic, and porcelain mixing bowls as these will probably work best. You will need larger bowls as your child grows. When she can sit up by herself, she is ready to move up to a potty chair.

First-Class Potties

Buy your child a potty chair, not a potty seat. Look for a model with a base that is as wide or wider than the top so it won't tip over as easily. Before you buy, check for stability by having your child sit on it and lean in all directions.

Avoid potty chairs with arm rests. If young toddlers lean on them or use them to pull themselves into a standing position, they can easily upend the chair and fall.

Avoid models with built-in splash guards, too. A splash guard is a plastic barrier attached to the front of the seat of the potty chair. It is designed so that when little boys urinate sitting down, their pee hits the barrier and is redirected into the bowl. The idea is to keep the room from being sprayed, but sooner or later children will bump the splash guard. The resulting pain can be intense enough to cause potty refusals thereafter. If you buy a model with a detachable splash guard, remove it.

Moisture-activated potty chairs are useful for training older babies and toddlers. A song plays when the sensor detects mois-ture, providing instantaneous feedback. Children are delighted, and parents know when to applaud. But beware! Babies and young toddlers are likely to twist and turn to try to locate the source of the sound and can end up falling off.

Traveling Third Class?

Potty seats affix to the top of the toilet, reducing the size of the hole in the toilet seat so children can sit on it with less chance of falling in. Although most parents apparently prefer potty seats—they outsell potty chairs—potty seats have some serious drawbacks.

Potty seats that allow unsupervised access to the toilet are dangerous because of the risk of drowning. Even babies and toddlers who can swim like little fishes tend to panic if they fall into water and cannot think to raise their heads. It only takes about two minutes for a child to drown. Most parents don't realize what is happening because their child never makes a sound. If you do use a potty seat, be sure you are present to supervise whenever your child is on it. Leave the answering machine on and don't answer the door. Keep the bathroom locked at other times.

Potty seats are associated with training delays and chronic toileting problems. If you do decide to use one, there are a number of issues to consider:

- Look for a model with flared sides for increased stability.
- Check to be sure the potty seat is attached securely and does not wobble.
- Be sure the clips that attach the potty seat to the toilet seat cannot accidentally pinch your child's fingers.
- Provide a step stool so your youngster can get up and down easily.
- Pad the floor around the toilet and the nearby fixtures to protect your child in case of a fall.
- Buy a potty seat with a footrest or build one.

> **Quick Trip**
> On average, children who use a potty seat take longer to be trained and have more toileting problems. Many youngsters feel less secure so high from the ground, which adds to their fearfulness. If they do fall off, it is hard to induce them to get back on. Without a proper footrest, they cannot push during bowel movements.

Despite the drawbacks of potty seats, lots of toddlers are indifferent to potty chairs and only become interested in toileting when a potty seat is installed. They enjoy climbing and like sitting high off the ground. Most of all, they revel in the chance to use the toilet like older family members. The motivational boost provided by a potty seat compensates for some of the disadvantages.

Travel Potties

When young children need to use the potty, they cannot delay more than a minute or two, which makes traveling a problem. To further complicate matters, many youngsters go through a phase of refusing to use anything but their regular potty. In that case, you can simply toss your child's regular potty in the car, line the potty bowl with a plastic grocery bag, and dispose of the bag after your youngster uses it.

Portable potty seats fold down small enough to fit in a diaper bag, making them especially convenient. Some portable potty chairs also fold down so they can be easily transported, and they are sturdy enough for everyday use. Before buying, check to make sure it won't accidentally collapse while your youngster is sitting on it.

A portable chair is preferable to a portable potty seat for use in public restrooms, where the loud noise and violent movement of the toilet water can frighten young children. However, it is possible to prevent automatic models from flushing by placing a piece of masking tape over the sensor on entering. Remove the tape after your toddler has left the stall.

Kids' Travel Guides

Dozens of children's books do an excellent job of informing babies and toddlers about the potty by explaining the process in words they can understand via characters they can identify with. A storybook can provide a good introduction and can help youngsters if they get stuck along the way. Even babies who have been reliably using the potty for a time tend to regress when they begin crawling or walking, and sometimes a storybook can reignite their interest. Be sure to buy at least one, and if your child doesn't love it, try another. When reading, substitute the potty words used in the story (*pee-pee*, *tinkle*, *wee*) with the ones you're using at home.

- *Caillou: Potty Time* by Joceline Sanschagrin (Editions Chouette Inc., 2000). This book is a big hit with Caillou fans. It can boost the confidence of tots who are so discouraged by accidents that they are giving up trying to learn.
- *My Big Boy Potty/My Big Girl Potty* by Joanna Cole and Maxie Chambliss (HarperCollins, 2000). These storybooks describe the challenges and joys of mastering the potty in a way that parents appreciate and many toddlers find inspirational.

- *Once Upon a Potty—Girl/Once Upon a Potty—Boy* by **Alona Frankel (HarperFestival, 1999).** At forty-eight pages, this story has more content than most, serving to instruct as well as entertain young learners.
- **Personalized Potty Training Book.** Enter your child's name and sex, then print out a personalized potty-training book at pull-ups.com. It's not wonderful, and you may regret letting your tot see the picture of a smiling child draped in reams of unrolled toilet paper. But it is free.
- *The Potty Book—For Boys/The Potty Book—For Girls* by **Alyssa Satin Capucilli and Dorothy Stott (Barron's Educational Series, 2000).** These rhyming books are favored by many kids. Parents appreciate that, unlike some books on the subject, the pictures show tots using the potty for its intended purpose in its intended location—not as a hat to wear around the house.
- *Too Big for Diapers* **(Too Big Board Books) by John E. Barrett (Random House Books for Young Readers, 2000).** Muppets fans love this one. Parents appreciate that it emphasizes washing hands after using the potty.
- *You Can Go to the Potty* **(Sears Children's Library) by Martha Sears, William Sears, Christie Watts Kelly, Renee Andriani (Little, Brown, 2002).** Pediatrician William Sears and his wife, a registered nurse, include potty-training tips for parents in the introduction and footnoted suggestions about how to answer common questions children raise.

The American Academy of Pediatrics advises against allowing children under age two to watch videos. Nevertheless, many parents have found that the movie *Once Upon a Potty* helps their child learn about potties and boosts motivation. Available in male and female versions, the film shows a cartoon girl or boy using the potty. See Appendix B: Resources for information about how to purchase a copy.

A doll can be a useful aid for helping toddlers understand the connections between drinking, wetting, and the potty. The Little Mommy Potty Training Doll comes with a bottle, diaper, wipes, and a potty chair. Other dolls that wet come with a baby bottle but no diaper or potty. You can solve this problem by using a handkerchief and affixing it with paper clips to serve as a diaper. For a makeshift potty, try a plastic measuring cup. Teach your toddler by walking the doll through the process of drinking water and eliminating, praising the doll for using its potty, and gently reprimanding it for wetting its diaper. During free play, your child

Question and Answer
Which type of hand soap and baby wipes are best?

Liquid soap is preferable. Germs can breed in a damp bar of soap, especially glycerin. The hands should be rubbed vigorously for fifteen to twenty-five seconds before rinsing thoroughly and towel drying. Avoid antibacterial soaps. Like antibiotics, they kill the weaker germs. Over time, stronger germs become resistant to the chemicals.

Commercial baby wipes are handy for cleaning up after bowel movements, but there is no need for this expense or the extra chemical exposure. Simply cut up old diapers or use inexpensive washcloths and moisten them with water. Place enough of them to make it through a day in a plastic box near the changing table. Soiled cloth wipes can be laundered with detergent and borax or enzyme bleach with the diapers. Or put some moistened paper towels in a plastic box and discard after using.

can use the doll as an outlet for potty-training anxieties and frustrations.

A simple song can help children understand the process of elimination and steps involved in using the potty. This one, which I wrote, is meant to be sung to the tune of "I'm a Little Teapot."

I Need My Pot
I just drank some water.
There's no doubt,
Under my tummy
It's hiding out.
When it turns to pee-pee
I need my pot.
Hey, lookie there!
It's coming out!

'Cause I used my potty
There's no doubt,
I wipe real good so
The germs don't sprout.
Then I take the paper
And toss it out.
I wash my hands
From the water spout.

I just ate some breakfast.
There's no doubt,
Under my tummy
It's hiding out.
When it turns to poo-poo
I need my pot.
Hey, lookie there!
It's coming out!

'Cause I used my potty
There's no doubt,
I wipe real good so
The germs don't sprout.
Then I take the paper
And toss it out.
I wash my hands
From the water spout.

5

Smoother Takeoffs and Landings

Reducing Jet Lag

When Darron was eighteen months old, his mother started getting him onto the potty each day when she thought he would likely need it. One day, she got the timing right. After a few more successes, training progressed rapidly. Darron went to the potty willingly and usually used it in short order.

Darron's mother worked long hours, so he stayed in diapers at his day-care center. At home his mother put him on the potty the first thing after he woke up in the morning, about ten minutes after breakfast, about ten minutes after dinner, and about ten minutes after his bedtime snack. On weekends she took him to the potty after meals and about once every ninety minutes at other times, setting a timer to remind herself. One weekend Darron had only one accident in forty-eight hours, and she assumed her potty-training days were about to end. But there was one problem. Darron didn't let her know when he needed the potty. She had to keep track of the time and prompt him every time.

To get Darron to take some initiative, his mother started asking him if he needed to go potty. Sometimes he would answer that he needed to poop, but he always said no when asked if he needed to pee. If she took his word for it, he would *have an accident. He felt bad about wetting his pants but didn't learn from his mistakes.*

Then Darron's mother came up with an idea. She set the alarm and taught Darron to turn it off. For a while she offered him the choice to go potty by himself or have her take him. Then she began giving him stickers and praising him when he went without her. "You can go potty all by yourself, just like your dad!" she would say. That pleased Darron immensely.

Still, Darron didn't initiate potty trips. It was as if he didn't know when his bladder was full. Finally, she came up with an idea for a game called "Beat the Clock." If Darron used the potty before the alarm sounded, he received a small prize. It worked, although she wasn't sure why. Perhaps Darron started paying closer attention to his body. Maybe he finally grasped that he could make the decision to go to the potty on his own. In less than a week, he finished training.

Timing is the all-important factor for fast potty-training takeoffs and smooth landings. Your child's first successes are likely to be "happy accidents": you simply manage to get the potty under your youngster at a moment when she happens to relieve herself. For your child to progress, you and other caregivers need to get her there at the right times so she can use it *regularly*. For faster landings, you must not let your youngster make the decisions about when to go potty until she is capable of making the right ones. Unless your child reliably asks to be taken to the potty or is responsible about taking herself, adults and older siblings need to remain in charge.

Your challenge is to be able to get a potty bowl under your infant, carry your baby to the potty, or walk your toddler to the bathroom at the correct moments. There are three ways to get the timing right:

1. Recognize the physical signs that precede elimination
2. Know your youngster's patterns of elimination
3. Have an intuitive awareness of what is happening inside your youngster's body

It is easier to tell when infants are about to eliminate than older children. After age four months, signs of impending urination, if present at all, are likely to be very subtle. Some babies pause and appear thoughtful. Some toddlers stand with their legs slightly apart and look down. Boys commonly have a slight erection before urinating.

Learning to recognize when your infant is about to eliminate is like learning to recognize when she is hungry before the loud wails begin. Infants seem to be attuned to their need to pee and poop, as evidenced by their restlessness and tendency to awaken just beforehand. Family physician Sarah Buckley realized when potty training her own infant that contrary to what is taught in medical school, infants signal when they need to eliminate. Buckley believes that if parents don't respond to the signals, infants eventually tune out the physical sensations and stop signaling to be removed from their bed—the same way starving children learn to ignore hunger pangs and stop begging for food. If parents don't start responding to their infants by age four months, infant-training authors believe that infants stop trying to communicate.

To learn to recognize you infant's signals, remove the diaper and spend time observing. Signs that elimination is about to occur could be most anything—a special wiggle, grimace, stretch, or reddened face. Listen for special gurgles and a sudden deep breath or other change in respiration. Some infants cry. There may be one type of signal before peeing and another before pooping. If you lay your baby on your chest, it may be easier to feel small movements, such as a tiny shiver or twitch. Write down everything you see and hear. Then, after your youngster pees or

> **Quick Trip**
> In cultures where infant potty training is widely practiced, experienced female friends and relatives help new mothers learn how to detect signs that their baby is about to eliminate. U.S. parents often have a hard time finding mentors to school them in the art of infant potty training and have formed online discussion groups to help one another. See the Resources section of this book for suggested websites or do a search for "discussion" and "infant potty training" or "elimination communication" to locate a supportive group of online advisers.

poops, go back and see which sounds and movements might have been relevant. Through continued observations, a pattern is likely to emerge.

Signs of Impending Elimination
- **Sounds:** grunt, moan, cry, gurgle, sharp intake of breath, sigh
- **Movements:** wiggle, tremble, turn of head, grimace, arched back, kick, jerk, increased restlessness
- **Other:** facial expression, sweating, flushed face, increased muscle tension, passing gas, yawn, change in respiration or heartbeat

Flight Patterns

To learn to recognize your infant's elimination signals and to get to know your infant's, baby's, or toddler's elimination patterns, you need to remove the diaper and observe your child for at least a day. Observing your child without a diaper can get very messy. Lay your infant or baby on a diaper or towel. Keep another cloth close by to lay over a baby boy in case he begins spraying the room. Cordon off the kitchen or another uncarpeted room to contain a mobile baby, toddler, or preschooler. Rather than observing your child during a single daylong marathon, it might be easier to spend several blocks of time together. You might schedule a morning observation one day, an afternoon observation on another day, and an evening observation on another. Plan some activities you can do together.

When your child unexpectedly starts spraying the room, be careful how you react. Contain your urge to shriek, shout, and scurry about as you dive for cover, especially if you are observing an infant or baby. Loud noises and sudden movements can startle your child. When startled, youngsters' muscles tense. The sphincter muscles tense as well, sometimes enough to stop the flow of waste. If shouting doesn't stop their child from peeing or pooping, many parents continue racing about until they manage to toss a diaper or towel over their youngster or he finishes eliminating. Then they calm down.

By startling their infant or baby when the diaper is off, parents unwittingly train their youngster not to eliminate when their bottom is bare. Once trained, the muscles remain locked in an effort to prevent waste from escaping whenever the diaper or underwear is removed. This can create difficulties during potty training. Many babies and toddlers sit on the potty for long periods with a full bladder but cannot eliminate. As soon as the potty sit ends and their diaper, training pants, or underwear is back on, the pelvic floor muscles relax, the sphincters open, and the youngster has an accident. See Appendix A for suggestions on reversing this type of sphincter conditioning.

Observing children naked to learn their patterns is messy, but babies and toddlers benefit from these observation periods. Many

> **Quick Trip**
>
> When observing your toddler to try to detect the signs that pre-cede elimination and to learn her elimination patterns, keep the potty chair close by. After your toddler has had several chances to see herself eliminating, suggest that she walk to the potty and sit on it the next time she starts to pee. If she doesn't, hold the potty bowl under her and try to catch some of her pee in it. In this way, you can start helping your child under-stand that the goal is for her to put her pee in the potty.

youngsters have never witnessed what goes on beneath their dia-per. Toddlers need to see themselves peeing and pooping to understand the process of elimination and to begin to compre-hend the goal of potty training: to learn to put their pee and poop into the potty instead of their diaper. You can keep the potty close by and suggest your toddler sit down and try to use it when he starts to eliminate, but most children cannot stop once they have started. If they haven't seen themselves eliminating before, they are usually too mesmerized to listen or respond to instructions.

Flight Schedules

Whether or not you are able to reliably detect when your child is about to pee or poop, knowing his patterns can help you antic-ipate his potty needs. While observing your youngster without a diaper, note when he eats or drinks and enter the time on a day planner, calendar, or chart. Keep track of when he urinates and has bowel movements. Calculate how much time goes by after meals and snacks before he pees or poops. Determine how often he passes waste when he hasn't had anything to eat or drink. Note whether he is wet or dry on awakening from naps and in the morning.

It may be helpful to keep track of exactly what your child consumes and when so you can identify any foods and beverages that are causing problems. Allergies and sensitivities to particular foods and food additives can cause digestive difficulties or irritate the bowel or bladder. The result can be constipation, diarrhea, or frequent urination. Food and food additive allergies and sensitivities can also cause behavioral changes, such as crankiness and hyperactivity, that make potty training more difficult.

Not every child has clear-cut patterns for eliminating; some youngsters are very irregular. Nevertheless, infants commonly eliminate during or immediately after a feeding. In fact, they are likely to eliminate several times in the first hour after a feeding. If your toddler has a bowel movement at about the same time each day or predictably urinates within ten or fifteen minutes of drinking, you will know when a potty trip is in order. Remember that children's patterns change as they mature.

When you start holding the potty under your infant, putting your baby on the potty, or walking your toddler to the potty chair, record the times of each successful potty use and of each accident. Keep notes about special circumstances and events that might help you get your child to the potty at the right time in the future. For instance, intense excitement, vigorous exercise, or drinking a caffeinated beverage may hasten your youngster's need for the potty. If your infant commonly begins urinating as soon as you remove her clothes in preparation for the potty, wait to undress her until you have the potty ready. If your baby typically rejects the potty before a nap, crankiness may be the problem, so an earlier naptime may help.

Many older untrained youngsters seem to have a hard time recognizing the signals their body sends that the time to pee or poop is approaching. They can't readily determine when they need to use the potty during the day and don't awaken when they need to use it at night. When asked if they need to go potty, older toddlers may say no and then have an accident a few minutes later. Parents tend to assume their child fibbed to avoid a potty trip. But many children feel terrible about accidents and truly want to prevent them. Doctors believe that most bed-wetting occurs because the brain does not respond to the bladder's signal that it is full. Perhaps years of practice sleeping with wet diapers conditions the brain to ignore the bladder. Be that as it may, many toddlers and older children want to stop wetting the bed but cannot awaken so they can use the potty. By knowing your child's patterns, you will be more able to take her to the potty at the right times.

As you learn to identify the signals preceding elimination, help your child identify them. The process is the same as helping your child identify other signals, such as the need to eat or sleep. When your child's behavior deteriorates and you realize he hasn't eaten in some time, you say something like, "You're probably cranky because you're hungry. Let's get you something to eat." When your child needs to sleep, you probably say, "You're wound up because you're tried. Let's get you to bed." Similarly, when you notice signs that your child might need to eliminate and he hasn't gone potty in quite some time, it's important to explain, "You haven't gone potty in a while and are passing gas. Let's get you to the potty and see if you need to use it." This helps to build sensory awareness.

Flying Blindfolded

Your intuition can also help you determine when your youngster needs to eliminate. Bonded parents share an intuitive (some would say "psychic") connection with their child that defies rational understanding. Mothers commonly startle awake when their child is ill, even though he is in another room and is not crying. They sleep through their husband's snores but hear the faint sound of bare feet padding across the carpet when their toddler gets out of bed in the middle of the night. As a result, many mothers find themselves running the potty to their baby, even though the clock says it is much too soon and their baby has given no sign of needing it. Yet they often discover that their intuition is correct. Time and again, parents learn that their unexplained hunches are better guides than mountains of data. If you have a sudden strong feeling or even a vague hunch that your infant needs the potty, you may be right. Similarly, if the clock says it is time for your youngster to use the potty but you somehow suspect he doesn't need it yet, you may also be correct.

Many Western parents are disinclined to trust their intuition. They have been taught to pay attention to information coming in through the senses and to ignore whatever they cannot see, hear, taste, touch, or smell. Author Laurie Boucke notes that in cultures where infant training is the norm, parents don't limit themselves to knowledge they can prove or explain and rely heavily on their intuition. Discounting your intuitive knowledge can leave you searching for tangible signs that your youngster needs to eliminate when there aren't any. Waiting for the correct amount of time to elapse instead of responding when your inner voice says that your youngster is about to pee or poop can lead to more accidents.

If you are unaccustomed to letting your intuition guide you, there are several things to try. Spend more time observing your youngster both awake and asleep. Study him carefully and try to imagine what is happening inside him. Another technique is to record your hunches about your child's need to eliminate when you chart his patterns, then review your notes later. Over time this written feedback may help you become more adept at recognizing when your intuition is correct.

Motivating Young Passengers

Introduce the potty slowly to help your baby or toddler become comfortable with it. Praise him for going near it, then for sitting on it. To encourage a restless tot to remain seated, you may need to distract and entertain him. As soon as your child is able to sit still, gradually phase out of your role as entertainer. Encourage your youngster to entertain himself by looking at a book or playing quietly with a toy. Focus your efforts on ensuring that the time spent cleaning up after using the potty is enjoyable.

Many parents hurry through cleanup chores, but this is a mistake. When children wear diapers, a lot of important parent-child interaction takes place during diaper changes. Children lose this special one-on-one time with their parent when they use the potty. Toddlers tend to cling to diaper rituals with an especially fierce tenacity. Even if they resist diaper changes, they may miss them, too. It is not surprising that after toddlers gain some experience using the potty, many decide they prefer diapers.

To help compensate your child, invent some special rituals. After potty time ends, sing a song, recite a nursery rhyme, or do both as you wipe your baby's bottom, put her clothes back on, empty and rinse the potty bowl, and wash her hands. Enhance the time spent cleaning up by providing a multisensory experience. Apply a squirt of cologne and a dab of hand lotion to replace the creams, powders, and ointments you applied during diaper changes. Little boys love the sweet smells, too. When your child has an accident and needs a diaper change, be matter-of-fact and businesslike during cleanup. Save the good times for after-potty times.

Chatting or playing with your child after potty time can help maintain your youngster's motivation during future potty trips. You don't need to say, "If you will sit quietly on the potty for five minutes, I will let you finger paint afterwards." Rather than trying to bribe your child, simply take your child to the potty and suggest a pleasant activity after cleanup chores are finished. Even though youngsters don't consciously relate their behavior to the reward, their motivation tends to improve.

Parents commonly give stickers, treats, and toys to reward potty-training compliance and encourage continued cooperation. Many children receive a boost from seeing a tangible indication of their success and are motivated to continue trying to learn. However, spending pleasant time with a parent tends to be about as rewarding as tangible prizes. As soon as a sticker is affixed to a T-shirt or a piece of candy has been consumed, youngsters tend to forget them. Often the main benefit of concrete rewards comes from the parent's positive acknowledgment of accomplishments as they hand over a small gift. Although some toddlers seem more motivated to work for tangible rewards, don't discount the value of your hugs and smiles! They have a powerful if unconscious impact. With that said . . . beware of showering your children with an endless stream of "Way to go!" "Good job!" and other kudos. Many children respond to the endless thumbs-up signs and praise their parents shower upon them like so much white noise. Praise is only meaningful when you issue it for a genuine accomplishment. Commending a child for wolfing down a piece of cake makes no sense. At best, your child will ignore such mindless compliments. At worst, she will take them to heart and develop a distorted sense of her competence. Whether you provide praise or prizes, distribute them with care.

- Say, "Good job!" until your baby or toddler is content to sit on the potty. Then increase the requirements for a reward.
- Say "Good job!" whenever your baby or toddler uses the potty because you set him on it at the right time. After he starts using it consistently when you put him on it, increase the requirements for a reward.
- Say "Good job!" when your baby or toddler pushes to try to eliminate when on the potty. Then, after she consistently

pushes when placed on it, increase the requirements for a reward.

- Say "Good job!" when your baby or toddler pushes and actually eliminates into the potty. After he consistently eliminates into the potty, increase the requirements for a reward.
- Say "Good job!" when your baby or toddler communicates her need for the potty. After she consistently does that, increase the requirements for a reward.
- Say "Good job!" when your baby or toddler communicates his need for the potty and actually uses it once he gets there. After he consistently does that, increase the requirements for a reward.

Until using the potty has become routine, don't forget to praise your child often for staying clean and dry. And as your potty-training journey draws to a close, don't forget to praise yourself. You, too, deserve a reward!

High-Altitude Attitudes

Most potty-training books advise parents not to let their child know that they dislike messy diapers or consider accidents a problem. Communicating disapproval, experts say, might create too much pressure to learn to use the potty, erode youngsters' self-esteem, cause them to feel embarrassed about elimination, and make them ashamed of their bodies.

In actuality, mistakes during potty training are a normal part of learning, and patience and kindness are essential. However, sending mixed messages by pretending not to mind accidents when you really do can backfire. Sensitive tots can readily tell when their parents are disturbed. They commonly react to unspoken tensions by becoming more stressed and anxious.

Meanwhile, children who do not readily tune into their parents' feelings may fail to comprehend that accidents are undesirable. Such youngsters may decide there is really no reason to bother using the potty when eliminating in diapers is easier.

Scientists used to believe that children automatically develop an aversion to waste around age two. But now there are many untrained three- and four-year-olds, and parents commonly report that their untrained child doesn't mind the feel or smell of wet and messy diapers. Many youngsters don't notify their parents when they need to be changed. Even though they are sitting in poop and pee is running down their legs, they resist being cleaned up. They don't want to clean themselves up, either. Their lack of motivation to stay clean and dry makes them difficult to potty train.

Wearing dirty diapers for several years may desensitize children. Change wet and soiled diapers, and clean up accidents immediately. Parents have a duty to keep their youngsters clean and dry until they can handle the job themselves. Do not leave a helpless child in his filth. If your baby or toddler protests diaper changes, let him thrash and wail if he feels the need, but do not postpone changing him. Be sympathetic and reassuring about your toddler's accidents, but insist that he help clean them up.

Don't allow your child to play with her waste. The desire to explore this fascinating substance is normal, and most tots manage to get their hands in it. When they do, they enjoy squeezing, smearing, smelling, and even tasting. Toddlers are apt to be possessive of their little piles, regarding them as personal possessions. Harshness is uncalled for—little ones simply cannot comprehend the dangers. But you need to disallow this type of play. Say, "No! That will make you sick!" and wash your youngster's hands immediately. Supervise repeat offenders carefully and supply them with gooey, slimy substitutes: clay, finger paints, or a box of sand and pail of water.

Whether an aversion to waste is learned or innate, the question is how to help a child who does not mind wet and soiled diapers avoid them. Consider that most elementary school children regard chicken claws, cow intestines, and fish eyes as very gross because they have been taught that such foods are repulsive and should not be eaten. Children's negative reactions are not innate—these dishes are high in protein and are treated as delicacies in some cultures. Disgust develops from seeing the negative reactions of others in real life and on television, in movies, and in books. Curling up your nose when messy diapers smell unpleasant, handling waste gingerly, and expressing concern about stains and odors may help your youngster develop a similar aversion. Seeing your reactions can help an older untrained toddler understand his peers' dislike of smelly clothing so that he can comprehend the importance of avoiding accidents if he can and of changing into clean clothes immediately when he can't.

Youngsters should be able to develop an aversion to waste without feeling disgusted with themselves. Most children find the sight of dirty dishes and the remains of meals sitting on tables at fast-food restaurants a bit disgusting, but that doesn't stop them from wolfing down Big Macs. Teaching children that food lying on the sidewalk is dirty and must not be consumed or even touched doesn't teach them to feel ashamed of eating. Similarly, you can help your toddler develop a healthy appreciation for elimination and an aversion to waste. Teach her that peeing and pooping is healthy and normal but that wearing dirty diapers and touching human waste are no-no's. Disliking the smell and feel of wet and soiled diapers motivates children to learn to use the potty.

Being honest about your reactions while remaining considerate of your child's feelings may be the best policy. When you find your toddler playing with his waste, it is important to say, "Don't touch! That is a no-no!" just as when your child runs into the

> **Quick Trip**
>
> Many toddlers feel too ashamed of eliminating to let their parents know when they need to use the potty. Shame causes some children to hide when they need to relieve themselves. Many proceed to play with their poop, unaware of the dangers. Don't criticize your child's body or make fun of him when he eliminates, and prevent older siblings from teasing him. At the same time, teach that poopy diapers smell bad, wet diapers harm the skin, and touching waste is a no-no because it can make him sick.

street you say, "Come back! That is a no-no!" It is reasonable to tell your toddler, "Mommy doesn't like accidents; I want you to put your pee and poop in the potty" just as you say, "Mommy doesn't like toys left on the floor; I want you to put them in your toy box." If your youngster is already intent on learning to use the potty, reassure him that learning takes time and that you are not angry with him. Even if your child seems disinterested in avoiding accidents, describe what you will do to help him improve. You might promise to take him to the potty more often, remind him to aim so the spray ends up in the potty instead of on the floor, or let him go around bare-bottomed so he can get to the potty faster.

Helping clean up messes can give toddlers something positive to do, teach about proper hygiene, and relieve their guilt about accidents. Have your toddler fetch a sponge, hold the towel until you are ready to use it, start removing wet clothing, or help redress himself. If he has a tantrum instead of helping out, avoid sending him to time-out. Say, "We need to get this cleaned up so it doesn't stain the carpeting and make it smell bad" or "We need to mop up this puddle so someone doesn't slip and fall." Let the tantrum run its course while you mop and scrub. Maybe next time he will cooperate with cleanup.

Tour Operator's Survival Guide

When serving as your child's guide during the journey into potty land, there are some dos and don'ts to consider.

Make decisions based on your individual child's needs. The one-method-fits-most approach presented in books (including this one) needs to be modified to fit your child's temperament and personality, as well as your family's lifestyle. Every tot is different.

• **Remain flexible.** W.C. Fields said it best: "If at first you don't succeed, try, try, again. Then quit. There's no use being a damn fool about it." Once you attempt a new method, be sure to give it a fair try. But if it clearly isn't helpful, try something else.

• **Be realistic about what your child can accomplish.** Children's physical, intellectual, emotional, and social maturity set limits on what they can achieve at any given point in time. If your child lacks the motor control to pull down his pants, you must do it for him. If he regresses and needs to be a baby for a time so he can regroup before forging ahead, you must take over. While it's important to expect success, it's equally important to remain realistic.

• **Make potty training a family project.** Find ways for other family members to participate. Ask for their suggestions and solicit their help. If you run into problems while potty training, carefully consider the advice of your other children. Youngsters who have recently been through training often have valuable perspectives on problems they recently confronted themselves.

As witnesses to what goes on during a sibling's potty training with less stake in the outcome, they may be more objective.

• **Take care of you.** You really are your child's most precious asset. Keeping your youngster clean and dry, and teaching him to keep himself clean and dry, are a lot of work. Be gentle with yourself.

Question and Answer
Which kind of rewards are best for potty training?

Smiles, hugs, kisses, and caresses are best for an infant. Spend pleasant time afterward with a baby or young toddler.

If you must offer a bribe to garner cooperation, a small piece of candy or bite of sugar-coated cereal can be effective. Small cars are big hits with toddlers and preschoolers. Delayed rewards, such as being allowed to ride a mechanical horse on the next trip to the grocery store, tend to be less effective. Even a big reward may not motivate your child if it takes a long time to earn. It depends on the child. When one youngster was promised a new bike if he stayed dry for a week, he immediately got with the potty program and was instantly trained. Another decided that a bike wasn't such a big deal after all.

6

Advance Reservations

Lessons for Infants
(Zero to Six Months)

*Rebecca's son wasn't out of diapers until age four and contin-
ued to wet the bed until age six. Getting him potty trained was
an exercise in frustration that lasted for years. After learning
about infant potty training, Rebecca decided to try it with her
next child.*

*When Rebecca brought Devine home from the hospital, they
stayed in bed together for the first two days. Rebecca spent most
of the time studying her daughter to learn her elimination
habits. As Rebecca expected, detecting when Devine was about
to poop was straightforward enough. What surprised Rebecca
was how easy it was to tell when Devine was going to pee. She
grew notably restless, then suddenly stilled and began urinating about ten seconds later. Those first two days, Rebecca was
able to get a little pot under Devine in time to catch her waste.
Rebecca faithfully said "sss" while her daughter peed or pooped
to focus her attention and start teaching her what was
happening.*

*When Rebecca got out of bed on the third day, a comedy of
errors ensued but she didn't find it funny. She had bought a
sling but couldn't figure out how to wrap Devine in it. Once
Rebecca managed, she couldn't get Devine out fast enough to
avoid getting soaked. Rebecca abandoned the sling. She laid*

Devine on a waterproof pad and tried to keep an eye out for her signals while doing other chores. Rebecca invariably missed Devine's signals. The result was a mess from all the wetting and soiling.

Rebecca started dressing Devine in a diaper and only removed it while nursing. Rebecca held a pot between her thighs to catch the waste while feeding her daughter and made the "sss" sound when Devine peed or pooped. One afternoon about a month later Rebecca realized that Devine was overdue for a diaper change. When Rebecca checked, the diaper was still dry. On an impulse she carried Devine to the bathroom, held her over the sink, and made the "sss" sound. Devine squirmed, grew very still, and started to pee about ten seconds later. Rebecca was sure it was a coincidence. Nevertheless, when Devine's diaper was dry an hour later, Rebecca again cued Devine by saying "sss" and was astounded when she again peed in the sink. After that, Devine began peeing regularly on cue. The secret, Rebecca discovered, was to cue Devine to use the potty before she had an accident.

When Devine was four months old, she started crying whenever her mother forgot to take her to the potty during the day and when she needed to use it at night. If Rebecca hurried, she could get a pot under her daughter in time to avoid an accident. At age six months, Devine stopped wearing diapers altogether.

U.S. parents typically respond to their infant's cries by checking to see whether he is hungry, needs a diaper change, or needs to be burped. They check for a fever or rock or carry him. It never occurs to them that their infant might be alerting them that he is about to eliminate. Information about newborns' ability to help themselves stay clean and dry has been lost in just a handful of generations.

The notion that infants signal before wetting or soiling sounds ludicrous to most U.S. adults. They assume that infants only get upset when their wet diaper has made them uncomfortable. In fact, infants' ability to detect when they are about to eliminate is probably innate. Many infant-training experts believe that keeping the bed dry has survival value. Infants' need for a clean, dry bed is unquestionably as basic as their need for food, warmth, companionship, and cuddles.

If infants attempt to alert their parents that they need to use the potty but they receive no response, the next step may be to summon help by crying, just as they cry when they are hungry, wet, in pain, or lonely. And just as most infants eventually stop signaling for food and comfort if no one ever responds to their wails, they stop signaling for help with elimination if their communications are consistently ignored.

The fact that infants attempt to alert their parents when they need to eliminate and that they can be potty trained is not new information. In his 1928 book, *Psychological Care of Infant and Child*, the eminent psychologist John Watson urged parents to start catching their babies' waste in a potty regularly in the first weeks of life instead of waiting until age three months, as was the custom at the time. Watson believed that early training would speed the process of conditioning infants' sphincter muscles to release waste on cue.

According to a 1977 article by deVries and deVries that appeared in *Pediatrics*, mothers of the Digo tribe in east Africa begin working with infants at age two to three weeks. Their babies learn to urinate on cue by four to five months and have full bowel control by twelve months. In their 1957 book *Patterns of Child Rearing*, authors Sears, Maccoby, and Levin note that when babies started bowel training around the age of five months, the average child had full control at the age of thirteen months.

> **Quick Trip**
> The classic tome *Infant Potty Training* by Laurie Boucke provides an in-depth look at the history of infant training, describes how parents around the world train their infants, and gives tips for minimizing the mess while caring for diaperless babies in modern homes. It is a valuable aid for parents.

Researchers Timothy R. Schum, Timothy L. McAuliffe, Mark D. Simms, James A. Walter, Marla Lewis, and Ron Pupp noted in their investigation entitled "Factors Associated with Toilet Training in the 1990s" that it is biologically possible to train infants to control their sphincters voluntarily and postpone elimination for short periods by three to six months old with behavioral-shaping techniques. Nevertheless, medical students are routinely taught that infants have no control over elimination.

Most experts on potty training toddlers are markedly unaware of what is involved in working with infants. When authors mention infant potty training at all, it is usually during discussions of the harsh methods some parents used to train older children in the past. Such authors seem unaware that infants are active participants in the process and that no coercion or force is involved. Moreover, most authors state that because infant potty training involves catching a child's waste in a pot, parents end up trained, not the infants. In actuality, catching your baby's waste in a pot is only one aspect of training.

Family physician Sarah Buckley recounted her experiences potty training her infant in an article titled "Mothering, Mindfulness and a Baby's Bottom" (copyright March 2002), which can be viewed at womenofspirit.asn.au/docs/sbmindovermatter.txt. Buckley describes how simple and painless the process of infant training can be in this adaptation of her original article:

I had read in a letter to *Mothering* magazine that African women cue their babies to wee and poo with a "psss" sound, and I did this with Maia, my fourth baby, from birth. This practice made sense to me because it felt closer to our genetic imprint, and I was drawn to the idea of a deeper physical and psychic connection with my baby. When I first learned about elimination communication, Maia was three months old. I held her over the laundry tub and made the "psss" sound; to my delight, she weed straight away, and we began our practice of elimination communication. As a family physician, the physiology of elimination communication is totally counter to what I had been taught at medical school, where it was asserted that babies do not have sphincter control until close to the second birthday. Obviously the paediatricians didn't consult the global majority of mothers, for whom knowing their babies' elimination needs is as simple as knowing their own.

I've come to the conclusion that probably ALL babies signal their elimination needs from an early age, but because parents are not listening, they misinterpret the signals as tiredness, needing to feed, or just crankiness, especially if the baby is in a nappy and the connection with eliminating is not observed.

Infant-Training Benefits

Learning your infant's elimination patterns, recognizing his advance warning signals, and catching waste in a pot to keep him clean and dry can help you connect with your youngster at a deeper level. Communicating with your infant about elimination nurtures a more intimate relationship that is hard to achieve in other ways. In fact, the communication that develops is so powerful that many parents soon conclude that their original goal of potty training their infant isn't so important after all. They say that potty accomplishments pale in comparison to the other benefits: the enhanced relationship that comes from their deepened

Quick Trip

Even if you have a hard time recognizing your baby's need to eliminate in advance and can't get a little pot to her in time, you can still do infant potty training. If you can't readily detect your baby's signals in advance, you can still teach her to understand yours. Whenever you observe her eliminating, start making a special sound and continue until she finishes. If you can manage to do this several times a day, she will eventually comprehend. Then you can hold a pot under her when you think it's time for her to eliminate and cue her to use it.

understanding of their youngster and from dealing with a more contented child. Parents commonly report that parenting is less stressful and more pleasurable. Being able to enjoy their youngster in the moment makes them less anxious for her to mature and function more independently.

By ignoring your infant's elimination signals, you teach him to use his diaper as a toilet. You teach him not to signal for help until he needs a diaper change. Later, you will need to teach him not to use his diaper as a toilet and to let you know he needs to pee or poop in advance. Overcoming long-established habits and identifying sensations your child has ignored for years can be very difficult.

By responding to your infant's elimination needs before then, you provide your baby with a number of benefits:

• **You help your baby maintain sensory awareness.** Infants stay in touch with their bodies and remain aware of the need to eliminate when parents respond to them.

• **You help your baby exercise her muscles.** The sphincters open by reflex when the bladder and bowel are too full, releasing waste automatically before potty training. Children learn to willfully open the sphincters during training.

- **Your parenting improves.** Pediatrician William Sears points out that while working with newborns on potty training, parents learn to read their baby's body language.
- **Bonding improves.** Your responsiveness to your baby is likely to bring you closer.

Parents' Travel Dictionary

Whenever your baby is relieving himself, teach him what is happening by giving the same special sound to signal him, such as saying "sss," "psss," or "shshsh." Continue making the sound as long as he is passing waste and stop as soon as he finishes. Do this whether he is eliminating in a diaper or into a little pot. In this way, you call his attention to what is happening. The more consistent you are about making the sound when he is eliminating, the sooner he will learn to associate it with peeing and pooping. When he does, the sphincters will open in response to your signal. If there is any waste in his bladder or bowel, it will come out.

Sphincter training can happen in a matter of weeks if you signal very consistently. You will eventually succeed even if you are only consistent during bowel movements, since both sphincters are relaxed at that time. In a 1985 study of an American child who began training at the age of thirteen weeks reported in the *Journal of Applied Behavior Analysis*, conditioning the sphincters took only nineteen days. You will probably succeed even if you usually miss when your baby urinates and only signal about half of the time when she is pooping, according to the authors of *Potty Training Without Tears*. If your child does not signal clearly when he needs to eliminate, it will be very hard for you to catch waste. You may end up with many misses and rarely manage to signal when he is peeing or pooping. Do not despair!

Although your baby will learn faster if you signal consistently, he can still learn from occasional signals. If nothing else, leave the diaper off during and immediately after feedings so you can tell when he is peeing and pooping and can give the signal. You can make progress even if you only signal during bowel movements, when both sphincters are relaxed. However, you cannot train the sphincters if you sometimes signal when no waste is being released. You must only signal when your baby is actually relieving himself, whether into a diaper or a pot.

After you have been signaling while your infant eliminates for a time, check to see if she understands your meaning. When you suspect she probably needs to pee or poop, give the signal. If she responds by eliminating, praise her wholeheartedly. If she does not, continue to teach by signaling each time she eliminates. If you are consistent, she will learn. When she does, you can hold a pot for her when it is close to time for her to eliminate, then give the signal and catch her waste. Praise her heartily each time she eliminates into a pot, and she will soon be using it regularly.

Here's a step-by-step plan for potty training your infant:

1. Leave the diaper off as much as possible and say "sss" or "shshsh" whenever your infant pees or poops.
2. Try to get a pot under your infant to catch the waste.
3. Carefully stabilize the head and neck when holding your infant over a pot. Gently push down an infant boy's penis to keep him from spraying the room.
4. Continue saying "sss" or "shshsh" the entire time your infant is relieving himself and stop as soon as he finishes.
5. Kiss and cuddle your baby to reinforce him.
6. Wipe your infant's bottom with toilet tissue.

This phase of learning isn't really infant training, it's parent training! *You* must learn to signal at the right times. Once your

> **Quick Trip**
>
> Your child will learn more rapidly if she associates your special signal with the relief from having less bladder and bowel pressure, and the comfort of being cuddled and loved after she eliminates in the spot you designate. The feel of the pot on her bottom can also serve as a signal to eliminate, so using the same type of receptacle consistently may speed learning. Be sure to reinforce your infant by smiling, stroking her face, and spending a moment kissing and cuddling her.

baby understands and responds to your signal reliably, only give the special signal when your baby is eliminating into a pot.

Keeping records of your progress can help you improve:

- Record the times at which your infant passes waste.
- Note whether your infant urinated or had a bowel movement.
- List any special things your infant did beforehand so you can better read the signs indicating that he is about to eliminate.
- Note whether you gave your special signal while your infant was relieving himself.

Stress-Free Travel

In *Toilet Training Without Tears*, authors Charles E. Schaefer and Theresa Foy DiGeronimo discuss the benefits of training newborns. However, they suggest waiting until the age of three months to begin training. They point out that newborns' systems are very unpredictable. By age twelve weeks, infants urinate far less frequently and in larger amounts, and their bowel movements are more regular. It is easier for parents to keep up with them.

It is true that because infants pee and poop so frequently, keeping them clean and dry and protecting the household in the first month of life is challenging. Infants may urinate twenty times a day, and breast-fed babies average six bowel movements a day. Keeping up with them is easier when children eliminate less often, so some families prefer to use diapers and wait to begin training for a month or two. However, caring for a newborn is necessarily an all-consuming, round-the-clock endeavor. By starting at birth, you will have many opportunities in a short period of time to get to know the signs that your baby is about to eliminate, practice responding, and start preparing your youngster for the next phase of training. Delaying training for a month or two means your infant will probably need more time to learn.

It is obviously preferable if you can tell when your infant needs to eliminate far enough in advance so you can remove his diaper beforehand and get him to a receptacle without a mad scramble. For help learning to detect the signs, read Chapter 5. Even if regularly catching your baby's waste in a pot turns out to be too demanding, keep it close at hand during feedings. Infants often pass urine and stool while nursing or shortly afterward. If you are sitting down and cradling your baby in your arms, remove the diaper. Hold the bowl between your thighs and lay the diaper over it. When you see that your infant is about to relieve herself, quickly pull the diaper away.

If you want to keep your infant in a diaper, the type with Velcro closures is easy to remove quickly. If your infant starts eliminating while you are carrying him and his pot is close by, pull the diaper away. Position the pot under him with one hand while cradling him in your other arm. You can also use a sink, bathtub, or floor of the shower as a receptacle for waste.

You can hold your baby in many different positions while she relieves herself. Learning to hold her comfortably while providing good support for her head and neck takes practice. If you are holding her over the bathtub or sink, try pressing the back of her head against your upper chest, supporting her body with your arms, and holding her legs firmly above the knees with your hands. You can also set a pot on the floor, sit down so it is positioned beneath your calves, and experiment with supporting your baby's body with your legs and holding her as she eliminates.

By holding your infant so that she is slightly bent at the waist, you put a tiny bit of pressure on the bladder and bowel. This may help to stimulate bowel and bladder contractions. Holding her legs securely makes it easier for her to push during bowel movements. Take care that you stabilize the head and neck and do not drop her! For ideas about holding techniques, see the photos at timl.com/ipt. Learning to hold your infant comfortably while she eliminates into a pot may take a while. You will improve with practice.

Some very conscientious parents strive to avoid using diapers altogether. They sleep with their infant so they can get a pot to him when he needs it at night. Catching waste at night can prove overly taxing; many parents simply use a diaper. However, your infant may awaken you after toileting in his diaper anyway and cry until you clean him up. Catching waste in advance makes cleanup much easier. Because your baby's sleep is likely to improve when you tend to his elimination needs, keeping him in bed with you and catching waste at night may help both of you get more rest.

In *Potty Training Without Tears*, the authors suggest that if you can catch at least eighteen bowel movements in a pot while making your special sound, and if your baby goes eight days without a pooping accident during a ten-day period, you are ready for the next step: teaching your youngster to signal you with a wave

> **Quick Trip**
>
> To enhance communication about potty training (and every-
> thing else), begin teaching your baby a bit of sign language. Ges-
> tures for words relating to toileting are in Chapter 3. The *Baby
> See 'n Sign* DVD or video, selected as one of *Parenting* maga-
> zine's best 2002 videos, can help you expand your vocabulary.

or another gesture so you can easily tell when he needs the potty. To learn how, see the section entitled Baby-Sponsored Trips in the next chapter. In the meantime, keep the potty bowl on the same side when your baby is not using it so she will learn to look or wave in that direction when she needs it. If your baby doesn't pass waste as usual after a feeding, or if she doesn't pee for a longer time than usual, quickly take her to the potty bowl and make the special sound you have been using. Perhaps she needs to go and is waiting for your signal!

Reluctant Travelers

Do not be surprised if your infant stumbles along the path to becoming potty trained. If she signals for the potty but doesn't use it, wait a few minutes to see what happens. Even older toddlers sometimes think they need to go potty, then realize after they get there that they don't.

Keep in mind that if your infant is ill, tired, cranky, stressed, or feeling a bit under the weather, she may forget to signal when she needs the potty or lack the energy to try to alert you. Hold her over the potty bowl, and give your signal when you know it's probably time for her to eliminate. Even toddlers don't always notice when they need the potty, or they notice but don't feel up to using it. Infants may at times be unable to pass waste in the potty bowl because they are too tense. Just as they get upset and push their bottle away even though they are hungry, they may reject the potty bowl and then have an accident when they relax.

If your infant stops signaling for days, weeks, or months, he may be ill, be upset over a household change, be distracted by family tension, or have forgotten how to use the signal, or he may be merely going through a stage. Continue taking the potty bowl to him when you think it's time, give your signal when he is actually using it, and add lots of cuddles and coos during and after each potty use. If something scared your infant while he was on, near, or looking at the potty bowl—such as a loud noise, a fall, or the sensation of falling—his sphincters may tense when you hold him over the potty so he cannot release waste. Try holding him over a different container, such as a bathtub, sink, or pan. Or try holding him in a different position. Both can relieve boredom and spark renewed interest in using the potty. Sometimes it is best to put potty training on hold for a time.

You cannot control your infant and should not try to force your infant to eliminate. Instead, strive to control yourself. Your job is to signal when your youngster eliminates and to try to learn his signals so you can present the potty at the right times. When you succeed, signal as he uses it, then hug and kiss him to express your approval. If you feel impatient or frustrated, stop potty training. Infants react to tension even when their parents try to hide their feelings. The sphincters may tense, preventing infants from releasing waste.

Being so attentive and responsive to your baby can be exhausting. If you lose your temper and scream or handle your infant roughly, put training on hold for a time to give her time to forget the incident. Nevertheless, she may retain the traumatic memory, in which case potty training may still turn out to be difficult in the future. It is critical that you monitor your emotions and take a break from potty training *before* you get to the point of losing your temper. It is better to send no signals than the wrong ones.

Finding support for your infant-training project can be difficult. Even after you explain the process to friends and relatives, some may persist in thinking it involves some sort of cruelty. They may picture an infant who can't even sit up being forced to sit on a potty chair. Usually their negative opinions change when they see an infant using the potty, so invite skeptics over for a demonstration. However, their guilt about making their own youngster lie in excrement may still cause them to debate your method. In trying to sell them on the merits of infant potty training, avoid criticizing their methods. Doing so is likely to make them more defensive.

Many pediatricians think infants' sphincter muscles are too weak to contain urine. Like trying to breast-feed back in the days when experts insisted that formula was better, you may not convince your child's doctor that this age-old, natural approach is better for your infant than diapers. Sharing some reading material about infant training may help.

If potty training your infant proves to be too messy, it may be better to just use diapers and give up trying to catch waste in a pot. It is more important to relax and enjoy your infant. Once she can sit up, you can try the baby track described in Chapter 7. Even if you think all your efforts were a waste of time, you may later discover that your baby learned a lot. Many parents say toddler potty training was much faster and easier for the child they worked with briefly during early infancy than for their other youngsters.

Question and Answer

My infant used to sleep through the night without a problem. Ever since she started using the potty regularly during the day, she has been waking up crying every night. Might the two be related?

If she seems comfortable with using the potty, she's probably waking up because she needs it. After infants are accustomed to being clean and dry, some have no tolerance for wet or soiled diapers, so once they stay dry during the day, they may try to avoid wetting and soiling at night as well. Like older children and adults, it is common for them to awaken when they need to pee or poop. You will need to take her until she is old enough to go by herself. If this seems overly taxing, remember that she should be able to take herself once she can walk and use it without assistance by age one and a half or two. Considering the number of children who awaken their parents in the middle of the night for years on end because they wet the bed and need the sheets changed, the time you spend now may be worthwhile.

7

Early Departures

Lessons for Babies and Young Toddlers (Six to Eighteen Months)

When Collin's mother said she wanted to start potty training him, her husband was skeptical. "He's only eight months old!" he exclaimed. "How would you go about it?" His wife demonstrated after breakfast the next day. She simply sat down on the sofa, put Collin's little potty on her lap, and sat him on top of it with his diaper on. She opened a storybook, and they looked at pictures together for about fifteen minutes. Collin didn't even seem to notice their unusual seating arrangement.

The next day Collin's mother removed his diaper and let him run around naked for a few minutes before inviting him to hear a story. Once again, Collin sat on top of the potty on her lap. A few minutes later, he gave a few gentle grunts, and began to poop. His mother grunted along with him as he eliminated. Afterward, she slathered on the praise and his father cheered. Collin obviously had no clue as to what all the excitement was about. Still, his parents' enthusiasm was infectious. He grinned from ear to ear as if he knew he had done something truly spectacular and gurgled with delight. He didn't care what that something might have been.

Collin used the potty eight times over the next two weeks, but only because his mother got the timing right. His mother

grunted as he pooped and said, "Way to go! You're pooping!"
The miracle happened two weeks later. Halfway through a
story, Collin's mother grunted softly. Collin began to do the
same. He then peed and pooped in the potty.

Collin's dad realized that Collin responded to his mother's
grunts the way sleepy people respond to someone else's yawn.
Yawns travel through a room, moving from one sleepy person
to the next, without anyone realizing that someone else served
as the trigger. Collin's father was amazed that teaching a baby
to use the potty could be so easy.

"Just a first step," Collin's mother said. "But a really big
one!"

The period after your baby learns to sit up by herself and before
she begins crawling or walking is in many ways the best time to
start her on the potty. The typically sunny dispositions of babies
make children in this age group a pleasure to work with. Their
social calendars tend to be empty, so they have plenty of time to
devote to the project. Babies adore their lessons, which are simply a series of fun games that parents and children play together.
Parents enjoy them, too.

Your baby is ready for potty training when he can sit steadily
and comfortably without help, which usually happens between
ages four and six months. If your youngster is still slouching, list-
ing, tilting, or needs to be propped up to keep from toppling over,
he's not ready. Use a potty chair, not a potty seat. Babies and
young toddlers need to feel secure, and being high off the ground
can frighten little ones—as well it should. They are more likely
to fall and get hurt. Check the area around the potty for possible hazards. If the flooring is hard, place folded towels or a blan-
ket around the potty to prevent injury. Even a minor bump can
make your youngster resist future potty sits. Once he can sit up

comfortably for a ten-minute stretch, you can start introducing the potty.

Working with a mobile baby or young toddler can be trickier. Once your baby can move about, he undoubtedly will be less amenable to sitting still on the potty. Even if he is already an experienced potty user, he is likely to get distracted after he starts crawling or walking. Many youngsters start having accidents even though they have been using the potty regularly for some time. Young toddlers may at times become upset when their parents interrupt their play for a potty trip.

Sears and his colleagues found that the youngest and oldest babies (ages five to fourteen months and over twenty months) were the least resistant to sitting on the potty. Children in the middle (ages fifteen to nineteen months) were more inclined to become upset. Yet Arnold Gesell's toilet training studies, which were reported in *Infant and Child in the Culture of Today,* found that children are particularly receptive to potty training between the ages of fifteen and eighteen months.

Even if your young toddler doesn't seem particularly receptive, working with him on potty training is important. After studying over four thousand children, researchers E. Bakker and his colleagues reported in 2002 that further delays increase the risk of problems with bladder control, infections, and increased urinary frequency. It is best to start training early and dedicate the time to helping your child develop a positive attitude toward the potty.

It is now common knowledge that babies and young toddlers benefit from many kinds of early learning experiences. Potty fun and games can help your child accomplish a number of potty-training goals:

- Become comfortable sitting on the potty
- Learn to eliminate into a potty instead of in a diaper
- Exercise the muscles used during elimination

> ### Quick Trip
> Modern potty-training experts warn parents against early potty training. But learning to eliminate into the potty instead of into diapers is like learning to eat with a fork and spoon instead of with fingers. Your child will need a patient guide to help her and regular opportunities to practice. Criticism won't help your child get food from her plate to her mouth without spilling. Her attempts to feed herself may seem hopeless when more food ends up on the floor than in her stomach. You will have to clean up many messes and continue to feed her yourself. Yet continuing to let her practice is to her benefit and cannot possibly harm her.

- Understand the word *potty*
- Become accustomed to toileting routines
- Integrate potty trips into her daily routine
- Communicate her need to use the potty
- Avoid long-term toileting problems

Rapid Transit

There is no way to guess how quickly a baby or young toddler will progress. A study conducted in the late 1950s, back when most U.S. parents routinely began bowel training early and tended to be more consistent, provides some clues as to what is possible. In *Patterns of Child Rearing*, Robert R. Sears, Eleanor E. Maccoby, and Harry Levin found that babies' progress varied dramatically. Some babies achieved bowel control in a matter of weeks; others required one and a half years. Here are the averages:

- When started between five and nine months, the average child had full bowel control at age fifteen months.
- When started between ten and fourteen months, the average child had full bowel control at nineteen months.
- When started between fifteen and nineteen months, the average child finished at twenty-three months.

These learning curves are a lot faster than the average of ten months many modern experts say that children under age two require. In fact, many researchers say that young children take longer to learn than older toddlers. That may be because researchers commonly classify children who begin training between eighteen and twenty-four months as early starters. Investigations of how children fare when training starts before eighteen months suggest that many progress more rapidly than children who start later. When Sears, Maccoby, and Levin reported the results of their study in the 1957 book, they indicated that delaying potty training until after the age of twenty months meant that the average child didn't finish until almost thirty months of age. Altogether, 8 percent of the babies that Sears and his colleagues investigated were bowel trained between ages five and nine months old, about 25 percent between ages ten and fourteen months old, about 25 percent between ages fifteen and nineteen months old, about 25 percent between ages twenty and twenty-four months old, and the rest thereafter. Back when this research was conducted, parents tended to be very conscientious about getting their baby onto the potty regularly. Most put their baby on when they expected that she needed to poop, said a particular word when pooping began, and praised successes.

Excerpts of parent interviews reported by Sears, Maccoby, and Levin in 1957 suggest that many mothers quickly realized that long, forced potty sits were too upsetting for babies. Fifty-two percent of mothers used no pressure or "slight" pressure. They showed their youngster when, where, and how to go potty. They

> **Quick Trip**
>
> Forcibly controlling children increases their upset and doesn't teach them to control themselves. Rather than trying to force your toddler to remain seated on the potty, serve as a role model by sitting on the toilet. Praise your child for sitting on the potty, even if her bottom barely touches it before she takes off again. Give her a book or small toy to play with. Refrain from conversation unless she is sitting down. Learning to sit for a five-minute stretch may take several months of daily practice.

took their child to the potty regularly but removed him as soon as fussiness set in. Some parents were much too strict by today's standards. They left their baby on the potty for as long as a half hour and expressed mild disapproval when a toddler had an accident. Stricter methods generated more upset and didn't seem to shorten the length of time babies took to finish training. Don't underestimate the importance of your baby's attitude. Your goal should be to make the time fun.

Preflight Instructions

Researchers Bakker and Wyndaele divided the thousands of children they were investigating into early and late training groups. When studying the children who had been trained early, the scientists found that half had started training before twelve months of age and half before eighteen months of age. Many of the youngsters were being raised by grandparents, which may explain why they had started potty training so young. The oldsters hadn't embraced the modern fashion of training late. The researchers examined their potty-training practices to learn the secrets of their success. Their investigations turned up some commonalities:

- The caretakers started training as soon as their youngsters began awakening dry from naps.
- The caretakers stopped using disposables when they started potty training.
- The caretakers instituted strict schedules for drinking.
- The caretakers followed strict schedules for putting their youngsters on the potty.

These proven strategies can help your child. So can a careful introduction to the potty. Be enthusiastic as you carry your baby or lead your young toddler to the potty fully clothed, saying, "Look what we have for you! Your very own little potty!" As soon as you set her on it, tell her how darling she is and praise her for being such a good girl. Cheers and applause will create a distraction for a baby, provide encouragement for a young toddler, and help a child in either age group decide that the potty is a fun place to be. Because babies and young toddlers don't understand most of what is said to them, your tone of voice is more important than your words.

No matter how enthusiastic you are, some youngsters are temperamentally inclined to reject anything new. Research suggests that such youngsters are harder to potty train. If your child is slow to adapt to changes, you can take the following steps to help him along:

1. Place the potty in your child's play area for a few days so he can see it. This gives him a chance to become accustomed to this unfamiliar object.
2. Invite your child to play near the potty by placing a stuffed animal on the seat, or make up games that encourage him to lift the seat or touch it.
3. Have your youngster sit on the potty fully clothed.

It's a good deal colder close to the floor and you don't want the chill to startle your child, so don't remove the diaper the first few times you sit your baby on the potty. After your little one has become comfortable sitting on it fully clothed, warm the seat with your hands before having him sit on it bare bottomed.

Chatting and playing will make potty time a positive experience for both of you. Try games you have invented or some perennial baby favorites:

- Patty-cake
- "Sooo Big!"
- "This Little Piggy"
- "Itsy-Bitsy Spider"

Cleared for Takeoff

Once your baby is comfortable sitting on the potty chair, start taking her several times a day when you think she likely needs to use it. See if you can learn to recognize the signs that elimination is about to begin following the methods discussed in Chapter 5. Signs can be difficult to detect in babies and young toddlers. Carrying a baby in a sling may help. If you do notice that your youngster is about to pee or poop, point it out. You can do this by making the American Sign Language gesture for *toilet* (see Chapter 3) and telling her what is happening in words, such as "You need to go *potty! Potty!*"

If you cannot detect signs that your child is starting to eliminate, concentrate on learning her patterns. For your youngster to have patterns, she needs to eat and drink on a schedule. When children graze throughout the day, it is too hard to predict their need for the potty. Make the American Sign Language gesture for *potty* (see Chapter 3) and say the word every time you pick up your child for a potty trip.

Whenever your child is peeing, whether into her diaper or into the potty, say, "Pee . . . pee . . . you are peeing" or whatever word you use. Similarly, teach her the word you use for pooping by repeating it while she is having a bowel movement. Unfortunately, it can be hard to determine when a baby or young toddler is in the midst of eliminating unless you can see what is happening. Before putting your child on the potty, drop a small piece of toilet paper in the potty bowl. Check from time to time to see if it is wet. If it is, or if she pooped in the potty, shift into high gear and let your youngster know how delighted you are. Strive to impress upon her that she has done something wonderful, even if using the potty was the result of good timing and she doesn't realize what has happened.

In *Potty Training Your Baby*, author Katie Van Pelt recommends that parents really ham it up every time their baby pees

Quick Trip

Once your baby or young toddler is using the potty regularly, gradually phase out of your role as entertainer. Instead, provide reinforcement after she is through. Review the suggestions in Chapter 5 for keeping your child's motivation high by praising her for new accomplishments. Shift the focus of your praise from skills she has already mastered to new skills she needs to practice. If she regresses for any reason, resume praising her for any previously mastered skills that are again giving her trouble.

or poops in the potty. She suggests being silly and trying to produce a spate of giggles. This motivates babies to try to get the good times rolling the next time they are placed on the potty. Eventually they figure out that the way to start the silliness that makes them laugh is to push to try to pee or poop.

Once your baby regularly pushes to try to eliminate when you set him on the potty, don't leave him on the potty for longer than a few minutes at a time. It is important to get him off before he becomes fussy. Ending on a negative note will make him more resistant to sitting on the potty in the future. End each potty trip on a positive note, and he is more likely to be glad to sit on it again.

Baby-Sponsored Trips

Until your baby can be counted on to let you know when she needs to eliminate, someone needs to take her to the potty at regular intervals. Once your baby can clearly communicate her need for the potty, you won't have to watch the clock all day long and life will become much easier. Hence, the next step is to work on your baby's communication skills. Actually, you can start teaching early on, as soon as your baby is comfortable with the potty, by following these steps:

- Keep the potty by your baby's side and within his range of vision, rather than directly in front of or behind him.
- Before taking him to the potty, tap it to get his attention.
- Praise him for looking toward it.

Repeat this procedure before each potty trip. Be alert to glances in that direction that might suggest your child needs to use it; some babies learn in very short order! Once your baby starts signaling when he needs the potty, you're well over halfway home!

The next step is to help your child turn toward the potty and reach for it with his hands. If you can tell he is about to pee or poop or it is time for a potty trip, quickly take his hands in yours and have him touch the potty while you say the word *potty*. Then pick him up and put him on it. If he uses it, praise him heartily. If he doesn't, simply remove him without comment. After some consistent successes, your baby will start reaching for his potty when he needs it.

After a mobile baby has learned to signal for the potty by turning and reaching for it, teach him to crawl toward it. To do this, keep the potty a few feet away from your child. When it's time for a potty trip, stand next to the potty and call him to it. Gradually increase the distance he must travel to get there. To get him to reliably signal each and every time he needs the potty, gradually increase what he must do to earn your praise. First, reward him whenever he signals to be taken to the potty. Next, only praise him if he actually uses the potty after he signaled to be taken. If he neglects to signal and has an accident, be matter-of-fact and businesslike as you change him. Don't be angry, but don't provide doses of tender loving care unless your youngster is upset about having made a mistake.

Quick Trip

Remember that rewards can be verbal praise or simply spending a few minutes of pleasant time together afterward. You don't need to tell a young toddler, "Because you told Mama that you needed to go potty, I'll read your favorite story." Provide more subtle nudges by keeping potty time and the time afterward fun. Let your child learn at her own pace.

Someone must be available to take your baby to the potty every time she signals and praise her when she uses it. You may need to teach child-care providers your child's elimination patterns and to recognize her signals so they can take her. Even if your young toddler can walk to the potty by herself, she will need help removing her clothes and cleaning up after she uses it. Have her help when you dress her in the morning and put on her pajamas at night.

Grumpy Travelers

Don't be surprised if your youngster wakes up one day and suddenly decides she doesn't want to have anything to do with the potty. Many babies and young toddlers stage what author Laurie Boucke calls a "potty strike." Youngsters who have been sailing happily toward the potty training shore suddenly disembark and decline to continue the voyage. Out of the blue, your child may object strongly when you try to set her on it, perhaps because she is tired, cranky, getting sick, simply doesn't feel like sitting there, or really doesn't need to use it. Often it is hard to guess what prompts babies to suddenly refuse the potty. Usually they are just tired, cranky, or getting sick. Their attitude improves during the next potty trip or they gladly resume using it again in a few days.

Some children start objecting to being taken to the potty each and every time, and they become upset when placed on it. Those who had been reliably signaling to be taken to the potty suddenly stop and go back to having regular accidents. It is not always possible to identify the reason for the regression. Just as the baby who loved peas suddenly refuses them, cries if a spoonful is put in his mouth, and persists in spitting them out for no apparent reason, youngsters can suddenly decide they don't want anything to do with the potty. If babies know why they change their mind, they're keeping it a secret.

There are several ways to entice toddlers who would rather continue what they are doing than take time out for a potty sit. Sometimes a change of scenery is helpful to woo a balky baby back on track:

- Hold your child on your lap with the potty under her and look at a book together.
- Sit on the toilet with your legs slightly spread, hold your baby on your lap, and use the toilet together.
- Let your baby relieve herself in the bathroom sink so you can make faces at one another in the mirror while she relieves herself.
- Hold your baby over the bathtub.
- Take your baby into the backyard to sprinkle the flowers.

Opinions vary about how to handle potty strikes. Back when U.S. parents routinely potty trained babies and young toddlers, the common practice was to continue the project through periods of recalcitrance and regression, according to Sears, Maccoby, and Levin. If babies stopped signaling when they needed to be taken to the potty, the solution was simply put them back in diapers and take them on a schedule again. In some families, the procedure was to carry the baby to the potty at regular intervals and immediately respond to objections by backing off. Other parents might require their baby to remain on the potty for a minute or two during each trip. Stricter parents kept youngsters on the potty until they settled down. Others were severe, going so far as to insist their child remain seated until he actually used it.

Modern authors advocate backing off whenever a baby objects. If a youngster regularly reacts by becoming upset, author Laurie Boucke recommends putting away the potty chair for a week or

> **Quick Trip**
> Research by Sears, Maccoby, and Levin found that a lot of baby distress and upset while sitting on the potty was associated with longer training times. Therefore, if you keep taking your baby to the potty despite his protests, dedicate the time to entertaining him. Don't encourage him to use the potty until he is again comfortable sitting on it.

two and returning to using diapers. If the baby's response is similarly negative when the potty is brought back, Boucke advises parents to put it away and wait a month before trying again.

If a potty strike continues for six months or a year, parents are understandably discouraged. But they usually report that even long-term strikes have happy endings. Their youngsters still show clear evidence of their early gains when they are reintroduced to the potty as toddlers. Even if they seem to be back to square one, their training proceeds very quickly and with little conflict.

Another approach is to continue taking your child to the potty regularly even if she fusses when she realizes where you are headed and wails when you arrive. If she continues fussing when you put her on the potty, try to distract her and cheer her up for a minute, then take her off if she doesn't settle down. Continue walking or carrying your toddler to the potty at regular intervals and encourage her to sit on it, but don't force her. Instead, close the door to contain her and sit on the toilet to demonstrate. There are some advantages to continuing to make potty trips even though your young toddler objects:

- The potty remains a regular part of your child's life.
- Your child learns that play must be briefly interrupted when it's time to go.

However, if your youngster is upset because of a potty trauma, continuing to take him to the potty may make it harder to forget so he can move forward. Ending each potty trip on a negative note may cause your child to become increasingly averse to being taken to the potty over time. If you decide to continue training rather than stowing the potty for a week or so, remember that "persisting" means taking your baby to the potty despite objections, setting him on it, and quickly removing him if he fusses. "Persisting" doesn't mean leaving him on it for long periods while he screams. Although it might seem that leaving a baby on the potty until he settles would teach him that he can handle the situation, a thrashing baby is likely to fall off. A young toddler would have to be physically restrained to keep him on the potty. Don't force the issue.

Question and Answer
My son keeps having one accident after the next. I'm wondering if he might have a physical problem. How can I tell?

Signs of congenital bladder or kidney problems include an unusually light stream (dribbling) or an uneven stream while urinating. Also, check for leakage after your child uses the potty by examining the underwear five minutes later to be sure it is dry. Such physical problems usually can be corrected by a minor surgical procedure.

Frequent urination can be caused by many things: food allergies or sensitivities, diabetes, a small bladder, medication side effects, or a bladder infection. Discuss the matter with your pediatrician or schedule an appointment with a pediatric urologist. Bladder infections can be dangerous and should be attended to immediately.

Don't become discouraged by a long period of potty refusals. If your child needs an extended break from training, many of the skills she mastered are likely to be evident when she finally consents to resume training. Even if all she can do is sit on the potty without a diaper for two minutes, she will still be light-years ahead of most older U.S. toddlers. Many two-year-olds are upset at the mere presence of a new potty chair in the house. Many two-and-a-half-year-olds balk and become hysterical if instructed to sit there. Many three-year-olds can't tolerate being without a diaper. Moreover, the training skills *you* mastered will undoubtedly still be in place. When you launch your child on another potty adventure, she will have the added benefit of traveling with an experienced guide.

8

Standard Schedules

Lessons for Toddlers
(Eighteen to Twenty-Four Months)

Diego's parents started scraping his caca off his diaper into the toilet bowl while he watched. They explained that his caca belonged in the toilet and he needed to learn to put it there. Diego's mother bought him a musical potty chair. She presented it to him when he awakened dry from a nap, figuring he would be more likely to be able to use it on the first try.

Diego removed his pants, sat on his potty chair for about two minutes, and then grew restless. At his mother's suggestion, he carried his chair to the living room and sat on it to watch television. Within minutes the potty's moisture sensors triggered a tune. Diego was delighted. When his dad took Diego to the potty a few hours later, he wouldn't remain seated and ended up having an accident. Then he had a tantrum because his potty didn't play a song. To calm him, his father finally put some tap water in the potty bowl. Thereafter, when his mother, father, or brother took Diego to the potty, he demanded tap water so he could make the potty play the song and refused to sit on it. Diego was a very bright child. He saw no reason to activate the sensors with pee when a few splashes of water would make the song play. Training stalled.

Diego's big brother decided that Diego could probably learn by watching and invited him into the bathroom. Diego imme-

diately jumped off his potty chair and insisted on using the toilet like his brother. They peed together. Diego didn't aim and made a mess, but at least he had used it.

After that, his family had all the usual toddler problems. One day Diego unraveled an entire roll of toilet paper. Someone forgot to lock the toilet seat and his mother found him playing in the water. Diego often forgot to aim when he used the toilet, so he left puddles on the floor and even sprayed the wall a few times. Nevertheless, he learned quickly and he was out of diapers in no time.

Around the world, children are potty trained in a time frame that fits their parents' expectations, according to Martin Herbert in his book *Toilet Training, Bedwetting, and Soiling.* In African cultures where children are expected to stop having accidents by around age six months, most babies stop having accidents at about age six months. In Eastern European cultures where children are expected to have good bladder and bowel control shortly after they can walk, the vast majority of youngsters have good control soon after they can walk.

It would seem very difficult for single and working mothers to find time to devote to potty training, but their youngsters finish earlier than the national U.S. average—close to age two, according to a National Public Radio report. Similarly, children of poorer, less-educated mothers finish sooner than youngsters from wealthier homes with more highly educated parents, even though children growing up in poverty tend to be slower to master other developmental tasks. A 2001 study published in *Ambulatory Pediatrics* found no correlation between the age for completing training and how much time parents spend at home. The high price of disposable diapers and burdensome workload of laundry may motivate poorer, busier mothers to move forward with training. It seems that the issue isn't the quantity of time parents spend at home.

Because most U.S. parents now believe that children lack control until after age two, the average age for completing training is now close to age three. Parents commonly blame slow progress on their child's lack of motivation. It appears that the real problem is that their parents fail to forge ahead.

Having expectations for your toddler's success doesn't mean you should pressure your child. Consider that babies can hold a spoon at the end of infancy but tend to drop it every time they reach for another object. They require many months of daily practice before they can actually eat with it. Even at age two, their grasp remains awkward. When they aim for the center of the mouth, they often hit the side instead. The minute they get distracted, the mashed potatoes end up on the high chair tray, tabletop, or floor. When getting peas into their mouth via the spoon proves too difficult, they give up and use their fingers. And the skills required to eat with a spoon aren't nearly as complex as those required to use the potty. It is understandable that children need a lot of practice. A lot of that practice involves learning to sit still on the potty and relax.

Quick Trip

Most of the world's parents expect children to finish potty training between ages eighteen and twenty-four months, and they do. At this age, toddlers should have the physical control to use the potty and the coordination to manage potty chores. They can get their clothes on and off, climb onto the toilet, wipe themselves, empty the potty bowl into the toilet, flush, and wash and dry their hands. Being in charge of these tasks is a big incentive for toddlers to use the potty and boosts their self-esteem. Don't shortchange your child. Teach him what to do, then put him in charge.

Unruly Passengers

When toddlers finally learn the maneuvers required to push out urine voluntarily, they can poop and pee even though they are a bit tense. Until then, the only way they can eliminate is by relaxing. Accordingly, they need to learn two sets of skills: the mechanics of using a potty and how to relax once they are on it. If you have a high-energy, strong-willed tot, you may need to work on mastering some important parenting skills that will help you do a better job of potty training—and become a better parent.

As a busy adult, you probably find that sitting is relaxing. When you take it easy for a few moments, you probably find it a bit hard to shift out of neutral and get yourself back into gear. For toddlers, downshifting and braking are more taxing. If your child's potty lessons stall, it is likely because his cruise control is stuck on warp speed. When you force him into neutral for a ten-minute potty sit, his psychic engines rev up instead of slowing down. He may be sitting, but he is probably wiggling. If so, he may be too tense to relax the sphincter muscles. If you force him to sit still for more than a few minutes against his will, he may start howling.

- **Be patient.** Avoid yelling and nagging to get your tot to sit still—that won't help him relax. Model by being patient yourself.
- **Be consistent.** Hold regular potty sessions.
- **Deal with accidents immediately.** If too much time passes between eliminating and seeing the results on the floor or in their diaper, children have a hard time making the connection.
- **Remain calm.** If your tot acts like you are a monster because you hold regularly scheduled potty sits, you need not enact the part. Model the correct way to express frustration by taking a few deep breaths when you are upset. Wait to speak until you can do so calmly.

- **Note and reward small successes.** Use smiles and hugs if you can, trinkets and toys if you must.
- **Set and enforce consequences.** Insist that your toddler adhere to potty-time rules. But also be sure he can cope with the rules you set.

Whenever your child is sitting still, point it out. You may be reluctant to comment, fearing that you will distract your child and your moment of peace will abruptly end. But toddlers need to know they are capable of sitting, and so do their parents. Healthy children are very active at this age, but parents who say, "He can't sit still for two minutes" are mistaken. Children sit while eating, playing with small toys, and watching television. Pointing out when your child is sitting still can reassure both of you that your youngster has the capability to sit on the potty long enough to use it.

An uncooperative, defiant child can turn a parent with the patience of a saint into a raging devil in short order. Rather than settling down and cooperating when reprimanded, a headstrong youngster may become more angry and upset. Both of you will be better off if you learn to discipline without resorting to heavy-handed tactics. The first step is to discipline yourself. Put your-

Quick Trip

Seeing others use the toilet helps toddlers overcome potty fears. Keep the bathroom door open so your tot can see you use the toilet regularly. The sex of the role model is unimportant. Dads can demonstrate for girls and moms can demonstrate for boys. Siblings can demonstrate, too. Firstborn children tend to take longer to train because they are likely to have fewer role models. Day-care friends often serve as their first teachers.

self on a regime of daily potty sits and have your toddler join you in the bathroom to observe you relaxing on the toilet. When your tot is ready for the potty chair, schedule potty sits when she is likely to need to eliminate.

Passengers, Please Take Your Seats

After watching dads mow the grass week in and week out, toddlers decide they want to do the same. The minute they are supplied with a small plastic replica from the toy store, they know just what to do. As they steer it across the lawn, they mimic their role model, even adopting his same expression, mannerism, and stride. Similarly, a good way to introduce the potty is to have your youngster join you in the bathroom once a day for a tutoring session, as well as at other times just to observe. Seeing peers and siblings use the potty also speeds learning and boosts motivation.

If toddler boys see dads and older brothers standing to urinate, the little boys will want to stand as well. Toddler boys need to sit while urinating until they can concentrate well enough to remember to aim, so sit to demonstrate. Show a boy how to push his penis toward the potty bowl to keep from spraying the room. When he starts standing to urinate, remind him to aim for the toilet and teach him to wipe moisture from the floor if he missed.

By setting aside time for daily tutoring sessions, you can teach your child how to use the potty and help him become accustomed to regular potty sits. Plan to dedicate ten minutes a day to the project. Tell your youngster that you need to use the potty and are going to teach him how. You will need several items:

- A book or magazine to entertain yourself
- A storybook (perhaps about potties) to entertain your child
- A doll that wets, a regular doll, or a stuffed animal

- A small plastic cup that can serve as a potty for the doll or stuffed animal
- A baking timer

Take your toddler to the bathroom and close the door to keep him inside. Set the baking timer to go off in ten minutes, and explain that you need to relax so you can use the potty. Tell him when you finish using the potty or the bell rings, the two of you can leave. Suggest that he look at his storybook. Start every potty practice session with a brief quiet time. Ward off conversation for one or two minutes by reminding him that you need to relax and use the potty. Suggest that he sit on the floor and play with the doll or look at his book while you read.

After a moment or two of silence, you may want to invite your toddler to stand next to you as you sit on the toilet and read him his book about potties or chat. It is important for you to remain seated and relaxed to demonstrate that this is important.

When you start to eliminate, explain what is happening:

- "Mommy is peeing. Can you hear it? I drank water, and now it is coming out."
- "Mommy is passing gas. Can you smell it? Oh, I don't like that smell."
- "Mommy is pooping. Can you hear it?"

When you are finished using the toilet, invite your toddler to help tear off some paper and hand it to you. Then have him help you flush, and wash your hands. Try to finish at about the time the alarm sounds. Do this every day for at least a week so your child can settle into a routine.

If your child has a hard time adjusting to new routines and is unaccustomed to limits, simply getting him to stay in the bathroom for ten minutes could take several weeks. If your child balks at attending a scheduled potty sit, carry her into the bathroom.

Quick Trip

The first time your child has a tantrum and you don't give in, he is likely to escalate his behavior to get you to do his bidding. The second tantrum may be even louder and longer. If you continue to hold firm, the third tantrum is likely to be milder—a half-hearted attempt to see if his proven method of getting his way is now useless. If you hold firm during a third tantrum around a particular issue, you probably won't see any more noisy forms of protest.

Explain that she has to stay until you finish using the potty or until the timer goes off. Try to distract and cheer your tot by making the time fun. If she has a tantrum, let it run its course.

Continue to hold daily sessions until your child has given up noisy protests, understands that she cannot leave the room until the alarm goes off, and has settled into a routine. It is not cruel to insist that your toddler spend ten minutes hanging out with you in the bathroom each day to play and read stories while you use the toilet. Don't let her upset convince you otherwise. Children do need to learn to cope with limits. When she recovers from each tantrum, commend her for managing to settle down. She may not be any closer to coping with the potty, but she's learning to cope with life.

Passengers, Please Remain Seated

When your child can handle being in the bathroom for ten minutes, she is ready for the next step. At the start of a potty sit, tell her you have a surprise for her and present her with her very own potty chair. You can increase the odds that she will be able to use it by giving her something extra to drink ten or fifteen minutes beforehand. For this potty practice session, you will also need to take a poopy diaper and a scraper, along with the timer, potty storybook, and doll, to the bathroom.

1. Set the timer as usual.
2. Explain that you put your pee and poop in the big potty, and her pee and poop go in the little potty.
3. Scrape the poop from the diaper into the potty chair bowl as she watches.
4. Give your tot a few moments to ponder the matter.
5. Then transfer the potty bowl contents to the toilet.

Model the proper way to handle the potty bowl so she can learn not to splash or spill. Show her how to remove the bowl from the potty. Carry the bowl with both hands, walk to the toilet slowly, center the bowl over the toilet, and tip the bowl. Then show her how to rinse the bowl and return it to the potty.

Sit down as usual to use the toilet and suggest that she sit on her potty. If your child takes a while to adjust to new situations, leave her diaper on unless she wants it off. You may need to help her undress. Either way, once she sits down, acknowledge her desire to imitate you and welcome her to the big-kid world: "You are sitting on your potty like Mommy, Daddy, your brother, Aunt Suzie, and Grandma Adams." Strike up a conversation: "Are you going to pee or poop?" Then have your usual minute or two of relaxed, quiet time. Suggest that she look at her storybook while you read, and follow your usual routine for the rest of the session.

If your child remains seated, is relaxed, and the timing is right, she will probably use the potty during the first session. If she does, help her get toilet paper, wipe, carry the potty bowl to the toilet, empty it, flush, rinse the potty bowl, return it to the potty chair, redress, wash and dry her hands, wipe up splashes, and straighten the towel. There are a lot of steps! Your child is likely to need many repetitions to learn them all.

If your tot doesn't sit on the potty chair, conduct the potty sit as usual. On subsequent days, continue to demonstrate how poop goes in the potty bowl by scraping a poopy diaper at the start of each session. Teach him to manage the potty bowl in steps:

1. Demonstrate how to empty and rinse the bowl (by doing it yourself).
2. Help your child empty and rinse the bowl (by holding your hands over his).
3. Turn the responsibility over to your child (by supervising while he does the work).

After the potty bowl is rinsed, follow your usual routine: hold a brief quiet time, chat, explain what is happening as you eliminate, and finish around the time the alarm goes off. If your child continues to avoid sitting on the potty chair during the next few days, suggest that she put the doll on it. It may help to rise from your throne and spend a few minutes showing her how to pretend that the doll is using the potty chair. Or find another way to encourage her to play with the potty chair so she becomes comfortable with it.

When your youngster can sit on his potty chair for a few minutes with a diaper on, hold the next potty sit at a time when he is likely to need to poop. Remove his diaper before the session begins and take him to the bathroom bare bottomed. Suggest but don't insist that your tot sit on the potty chair. But if you get a hint that he is about to eliminate or if he actually starts eliminating, tell him that his poop is coming and suggest he sit down quickly so he can use his potty like you. If he doesn't, let the accident happen. Explain, "There's your poop. It needs to go in the

> ### Quick Trip
> If your little boy wants to use toilet paper after peeing, let him. Teach your toddler how to count out three or four squares of toilet paper or measure a piece the length of his arm. Then show him how to keep the roll from turning by holding it firmly with one hand while tearing the paper with the other hand. Getting to manage the toilet paper is a big incentive to use the potty. Toddlers have to trade the comfort of a diaper change for burdensome potty responsibilities. They deserve to enjoy this small fruit of their labor. Yes, you can anticipate finding the house draped in toilet paper at some point. Tell your child that playing with toilet paper is a no-no.

potty." You will need to clean it up immediately. Sop up urine with a sponge and squeeze it into the potty chair bowl, explaining that his pee and poop should go there. Many children have never seen themselves peeing or pooping. Messes on the floor aren't fun, but they are part of the learning process.

Repeat the same procedure for a few days. If your tot continues messing on the floor, tell her you will teach her to use the potty like Mommy and Daddy: when her poop comes, you will sit her on the potty chair so it gets inside the potty instead of on the floor. Conduct some dry runs by exclaiming, "I think your poop is coming! I must hurry and put my baby on the potty!" Pick her up and put her on the potty, exclaiming, "Is it happening? Where's your poop?" If she is not starting to eliminate, say, "Oh, no! I was wrong! No poop is coming yet! Too bad."

When your child understands how this game goes and is comfortable playing it, play it when he actually does start to have a bowel movement. Announce that your baby's poop is coming and you must get him to the potty. Pick up your child and set him on the potty. After he uses it, hug and kiss him. Tell him that your baby used the potty just like you. Then complete the routine by helping him wipe his bottom, redress, empty the potty bowl, flush, rinse the bowl and return it to the chair, and wash his hands. Congratulate him on his great potty success!

After your tot has actually used the potty, you don't need to begin bathroom sessions by scraping a poopy diaper, but continue to conduct brief periods of quiet time at the beginning of potty sits and encourage your child to remain seated until he uses the potty. If he does, end the session after your child finishes cleaning up rather than waiting for the alarm to sound. Ensure your child gets the full ten minutes of one-on-one time by retiring to another room to play or chat until the alarm sounds.

On subsequent days, extend the quiet-time period very gradually. Try to hold off chatting and reading stories until your child uses the potty and cleans up. Make it a goal to change the routine so that playtime happens in another room *after* she finishes using the potty. Be sure to tell your child how nice and clean she is after she uses the potty, and how glad you will be when she doesn't have to wear wet, poopy diapers anymore!

Scheduled Arrivals

Once your tot is using the potty regularly during his single daily potty sit, bring out the big-kid training pants and tell him you will teach him to use them. You may want to continue putting him to bed in a diaper if he wets while sleeping.

Take your child to the potty when you expect her to need to use it, such as at the following times:

Quick Trip

Some children have problems making the transition from scheduled sits to independently deciding when they need to use the potty. Start asking your child if he needs to go when *you* think it's time. If he says that he doesn't, say, "Let's find out!" and take him. If he uses it, or if he doesn't use it and has an accident soon after, he might not have been able to tune in to the sensation of needing to eliminate. Make it a habit to ask him if he needs to go before taking him, so he can start concentrating on the sensations. It may help to touch his lower abdomen and ask, "Can you feel any pee or poop needing to come out?" before taking him.

- About fifteen minutes after she has something to drink
- After awakening in the morning and after naps
- Before bedtime
- Every one and a half hours after the last potty use or accident

Don't require a potty trip unless you think your tot needs to use the potty. Send her as often as you think she needs to go and as your schedule permits. Carry her to the bathroom if she balks, but don't try to force her to sit on the potty.

You can experiment with asking your child if she needs to use the potty and not taking her even though you think her answer is wrong. But if she proceeds to have an accident, don't get angry! She either can't tell when she needs to use the potty or isn't yet able to make good decisions about going potty when there are other, more fun things to do. Until she can do both, you need to make the decisions for her. That's really what child-rearing is all about.

Question and Answer
What is the best treatment for my daughter's diaper rash?

The guaranteed cure is to potty train her! Once she's out of diapers, she won't have problems. Until then, the trick is to keep her out of diapers as much as possible so the skin has a chance to heal. Even dry cloth diapers will chafe raw skin. So if she is very sore, let her go bare bottomed whenever possible.

To that end, remove a wet diaper immediately and let her air dry for a minimum of ten minutes. If she only wets once an hour, you should be able to wait for thirty to forty-five minutes before rediapering her—this is why it's so important to get to know your child's elimination habits. When cleaning her up during a diaper change, gently pat (don't rub) the skin with warm water to cleanse it or let her sit in a warm bath. Avoid wipes containing alcohol.

To dry her, gently pat the skin with a soft cloth or allow her to air dry. You can apply a commercial diaper rash cream, but most contain zinc oxide. Although such products do a good job of coating the skin to create a moisture barrier, washing them off requires some rubbing, which can cause additional irritation.

To moisturize, try pure aloe vera gel or vegetable oil. Simply pour some onto your hands and rub it onto your baby's bottom. For a powder, bake white flour in the oven or heat some in a frying pan, stirring occasionally until golden brown. Then cool it, and store it in a container.

The spores from the bacteria in urine are not killed during laundering with regular detergent. Use an enzyme bleach or add borax. Use vinegar in the rinse cycle to lower the pH. Better yet, let professionals handle the job, and sign up for a diaper service. The latter is the best bet for ensuring the correct pH.

9

Late Arrivals

Lessons for Older Children (Two Years and Older)

Kara started potty training at age eighteen months but wouldn't sit still or cooperate. Her mother tried again when Kara was two years old, then again at twenty-nine months. On the last attempt Kara worked her way out of diapers and began wearing pull-up training pants. But then she decided going to the bathroom was too much trouble and would put it off. Her mother would see her struggle to "hold it" by grasping her crotch, sitting with her knee pressed against her pubic bone, or jiggling a leg. At such times, her mother would ask Kara if she needed to go potty. Kara commonly said no but had an accident a few minutes later. Her frustrated mother threatened to put her back in diapers. Instead of protesting, Kara seemed relieved.

All of the articles Kara's mother had read said that a return to diapers was too confusing for children, so she hesitated to follow through with her threat. But after a few very messy weeks, she decided Kara just wasn't ready for the responsibility of training pants. A few months later, Kara came home from nursery school crying because some little friends had teased her about wearing diapers. She became very determined to learn to use the potty. However, she couldn't seem to do it. She would sit on the potty chair for as long as thirty minutes *while her mother read to her, but nothing happened. Soon after they gave up and Kara put her clothes back on, she would have an accident. She would cry, and it was obvious that she was trying her best.*

After piling up some more failures, Kara said she didn't want to use the potty anymore. The very suggestion that she try would upset her. She would set her jaw and refuse to respond. Her mother didn't know what to do to motivate her daughter to keep trying. If rewards were offered and Kara couldn't earn them, wouldn't that make her feel like even more of a failure?

For several decades, modern potty-training authors have been recommending that parents wait to begin potty training until after age two, and parents have been heeding their advice. In a study of toilet training in firstborn children in 1989, researcher Howard Seim found that more parents (42.6 percent) initiated training when their children were between ages two and two and a half than during any other period. Since then the mean age has crept up, and increasing numbers of potty-training articles recommend waiting until age four.

Some older children are so easy to train, they virtually teach themselves. They go from never having sat on a potty to being accident-free in a week. When that happens, their happy parents are convinced that they were wise to wait. However, the average training time for youngsters over age three is about five months, which means that many children require twice as long to learn. Some end up needing several years. Nevertheless, the more advanced development of older toddlers and preschool children can make for a faster learning curve.

Some characteristics of older children do make them easier to work with:

- **Advanced social skills.** Because older children readily learn by imitating others, they can absorb the mechanics of using the potty via videos, books, and dolls that wet rather than requiring a live model.
- **Advanced verbal skills.** Because older children can understand simple instructions, ask questions, and communicate their needs, teaching them is more straightforward.
- **Advanced motor skills.** Because older children can take themselves to the potty and manage clothes and cleanup with little help, their parents don't need to be as involved for as long.
- **Advanced cognitive skills.** Because older children can exercise better judgment, they can more accurately determine how long they can postpone a potty trip, making it easier for them to avoid accidents.
- **Larger bladders.** Because older children have larger bladders, they urinate less often. Most older toddlers only need to eliminate every couple of hours.

Nevertheless, it is a mistake to assume that an older toddler's better verbal, motor, and intellectual skills mean that she can figure out how to use the potty on her own. Children benefit from

---

Quick Trip

After having their bottoms continually covered for several years, many youngsters find the sensations of being naked startling and unpleasant. They react with fear and avoid the potty. For starters, have your child sit on the potty wearing a diaper. Warm the potty chair seat with your hands before your youngster sits on it bare bottomed, or buy a model with a cushioned potty seat.

being introduced to the potty slowly and being given detailed instructions about how to use it. Moving too fast can overwhelm your youngster. Many seemingly uncooperative children are simply confused about what to do.

Flight Simulations

Another advantage to working with children over age two is their ability to mimic others and learn from books and television. If you're uncomfortable serving as a toilet model, you may be able to make do with an alternative:

- Purchase a recommended potty-training video listed in Appendix B, "Resources."
- Find another potty-training video by searching websites such as amazon.com.
- Read your child one or more of the potty storybooks listed in Chapter 4.

A demonstration via a doll can be especially effective for children ages two and older. Buy a doll that wets or dress a regular doll in a tissue-paper diaper held in place with paper clips. Give the doll a real or imaginary drink of water from a toy baby bottle. After the doll wets its diaper (dab a regular doll's tissue-paper diaper with water) explain that the doll needs to learn to use the potty like a big girl so it can wear underwear and keep its pants clean and dry. Remove the wet paper, and redress the doll in cloth underpants. Give the doll another drink of water, then remove its underwear and put it on its potty (or on a small plastic cup). Praise the doll, wipe its bottom with a bit of toilet paper, empty the toy potty into the toilet, lower the lid, and flush. Tell your child you want him to learn to use the potty like the doll instead of peeing and pooping in his diapers.

Television star Dr. Phil McGraw suggests moving to the living room after the doll demonstration to celebrate the doll's success at using the potty. After the stuffed animal guests have properly recognized the guest of honor, Dr. Phil recommends telling your child that you will hold a similar party once he learns to use the potty. Children have a tendency, however, to assume that a single success is all that's required for potty training, so be careful to spell out exactly what your child must do to merit a victory celebration. So as not to give the wrong impression, you might make potty training the doll an all-day affair, perhaps having your child check the doll's pants and take it to the potty every couple of hours. You might offer to hold a celebration for your tot after he has remained dry for several days. Use a potty chart to track his progress toward the goal.

Some older children may be able to learn to use the potty without ever seeing themselves eliminate, but most need to see what is going on beneath their diaper. Having the opportunity to see themselves pee or poop helps them understand how their body works and the process of elimination. Follow the sugges-

Quick Trip

If the weather is too cold for an outdoor adventure, spend several hours in the basement, attic, kitchen, or another uncarpeted area of the house so your toddler can go about without a diaper and observe himself eliminating. Keep the potty chair nearby and instruct your tot to put his pee and poop in it if he can. It is not always possible to stop peeing midstream, but when your child starts to urinate, tell him to try to stop and hurry to the potty. Probably he won't know which muscles to use to stop himself from peeing, but it's worth a try.

tions in Chapter 5 and have your child spend a day bare bottomed. If the weather permits a wilderness adventure, serve lots of lemonade to promote peeing and provide lessons in the yard. Sprinkling the flowers and bushes delights youngsters and produces an instant attitude adjustment for those who have been nervous about potty training.

Hearing about the circle of life can help children age three and older understand how elimination connects them to other living things. Explain that when people pee and poop, they are getting rid of the parts of the food and drink their bodies cannot use. Their pee and poop waters and feeds the plants. The plants produce the air people need to live so they can water and feed the plants, and so forth. If the grass ends up being unexpectedly fertilized, use a paper towel and carry it inside. Drop it into the potty as you explain that this is where human fertilizer belongs until it is transformed into food that is fit for a flower.

Companion Tickets

When your child is accustomed to sitting on her potty and is ready to try using it for the first time, you might want to drum up some additional enthusiasm for this new phase of training by having her prepare the night before. Move her potty chair into the bathroom. Put some reading materials by the toilet, and have her put a storybook next to her potty chair. Lay out underwear so she can put it on in the morning. Encourage her to drink plenty of liquids with breakfast. Take her to the bathroom ten to fifteen minutes after breakfast.

Sit down on the toilet while your child sits on her potty chair. Explain that since she has pee inside, the next step is to let it out. To do that, she needs to relax her muscles. Often the best way is to think about something else. Suggest that she look at her book while you read.

If after twenty minutes she still hasn't used the potty chair, she is undoubtedly too tense. It is common for children in this situation to have an accident when they finally relax—typically when potty time is over. Standing up puts more pressure on the muscles, forcing them open. The goal will be to work with her on learning to relax. The following may help:

- Play a tape of restful music.
- Distract your child with stories or conversation.
- Listen to Jim Malloy's CD *The Complete Beginning Meditation Class* together.
- Read Sharon Penchina and Stuart Hoffman's book *I Take a DEEEP Breath* to teach your child about the calming power of breath.

Modern life can be very stressful for young children. Learning to relax is a valuable skill, and even two-year-olds can benefit from meditating. If the vocabulary on an instructional tape is too advanced for your child, listen to it alone. Then lead your child through a meditation session using words she can understand.

Quick Trip

Tell a joke! A giggle or small cough can help start bladder contractions and open the sphincters if your child needs to use the potty but is unconsciously tensing his muscles. Opening a tap to run water is unlikely to stimulate urination until your child has come to associate it with the sound of pee hitting the potty bowl.

Cruising Speed

Working with older children can actually be harder than working with younger ones. Although many two-year-olds are totally terrific, others display behaviors that show why the term *terrible twos* was invented. The negativity, defiance, and tantrums that commonly emerge as children strive for greater autonomy can create a potty-training nightmare. It can be hard to get youngsters to comply with potty routines when their favorite word is "no." And in recent years, the age of such difficulties seems to have moved forward. Conflicts commonly intensify when children reach what some parents now refer to as the "terrible threes." Because older children are more independent and less amenable to dropping what they are doing for a scheduled potty sit, getting them to comply with instructions can be harder.

News of classmates' potty-training victories and trophies such as new underwear and potty-training rewards can trigger troubling self-doubts in untrained children. Being teased by a classmate or sibling about continuing to wear diapers or disposable training pants can undermine self-esteem, causing children to feel like failures before they have even tried to learn. It never occurs to them that to graduate to underwear they must be taught. It would seem logical for youngsters in this situation to be excited when their parents inform them that they, too, can learn to use the potty and wear big-kid underwear. However, young children's minds don't usually work that way. They tend to shut down and avoid subjects that make them feel incompetent or ashamed. The solution is to move very slowly and make an effort to build your child's confidence. For instance, after the doll demonstration ask your youngster where he is supposed to put his pee and poop. If he says "potty" or points to it, let him know you are pleased that he is catching on so fast.

> **Quick Trip**
> A simple way to prevent fears of flushing and of being flushed away is to teach your youngster to close the lid *before* he flushes. Developing this habit can also prevent lifelong struggles over leaving the lid up. If your child is upset because his poop is gone and he wants it back, reassure him that there is more in the making inside his body even as he speaks.

The final stages of training older children can pose special challenges. When scheduled potty sits are phased out and the responsibility for going to the potty is transferred to children, they must remain constantly alert to the pressure in their bladder and bowel every waking moment. Like learning to move the foot from the accelerator to the brake when beginning to drive a car, new learners must pay close attention at all times before their response becomes automatic and unconscious. Until then, lapses of attention and judgment errors can readily result in accidents.

Other problems cause many two-year-olds to leap from the train before reaching their destination. For instance, fears of flushing are common in the middle of the third year of life, when many children become especially possessive of their belongings. Some potty-training experts maintain that children view their poop as part of themselves. Seeing it disappear down the toilet can raise troubling worries as to which body part might be next. Some pediatricians recommend waiting to flush until the child has left the room.

Scary urban legends spread as rapidly through nursery-school playgrounds as through middle-school slumber parties. Many members of the day-care crowd have heard about the child who fell into the toilet and was flushed away, never to be seen again.

Trusted pals relate stories of the monster (in some versions it is a snake, crocodile, or shark) that inhabits the toilet bowl and can unexpectedly rise from the watery depths to bite unsuspecting children while they go potty. The Mr. Clean television commercial, which featured a miniature muscleman emerging from the toilet bowl after scrubbing it to a sparkle, terrorized tykes across the country for years. When tots spread the horrifying news to their friends, tales of the little green man were later transformed by the minds of some listeners into the Incredible Hulk and a not-so-jolly Green Giant. Tales of the evil deeds of assorted toilet monsters continue to be handed down to new generations of children. If your child suddenly acts like you are sending her to her death when you put her on a potty seat, try a potty chair instead.

Parents as Travel Agents

By age three, learning to toilet should be a requirement, not an option, just like going to school will be a requirement in a few years. Still, you cannot force your child to learn in either setting. Hence, you may need to sell your child on this journey in an effort to boost his motivation. Explain that pee and poop belong in the potty, not in diapers, and describe how learning to put them in the proper place will benefit him. Mention the following advantages:

- Your child can wear underwear.
- Your child won't have diaper rash.
- Your child won't need to have diaper changes.
- Your child will smell better.

- Your child will be able to use the toilet like big kids and adults.
- Your child will help keep his bladder healthy.
- Your child's waste will be in the toilet where it belongs.

If your child remains less than enthusiastic, explain the disadvantages of diapers:

- Only babies and people with special problems use diapers.
- Dirty diapers are unsanitary and smell bad.
- Diapers cause diaper rash.
- Diapers are bulky, which makes them uncomfortable.
- Changing diapers interrupts playtime.
- Doing so much extra laundry is a lot of work for you.

The prospect of being able to wear underwear is a big incentive for most children. Consider letting your youngster select the type she likes. Explain that to be able to wear them, she must learn to keep them clean and dry. Your job is to teach; her job is to learn. To that end, explain that you will help her figure out when she needs to use the potty. Emphasize that once she can tell when she needs to pee or poop, there is only one way to keep

Quick Trip

You insist that your child learn to eat with silverware rather than her hands. You insist that she take baths. You also need to insist that she learn to use the potty, or at least learn basic toileting skills by cleaning herself up after accidents. Acquiring toileting skills is an important developmental task. In 2004, pediatrician Barton D. Schmitt noted in *Contemporary Pediatrics* that "using the toilet can enhance a sense of mastery and self-esteem. . . ."

her underwear dry: by going to the potty as soon as she needs to rather than putting it off. Extract a promise that she will go immediately when the need arises. Emphasize that besides causing accidents, trying to hold it can hurt her bladder. Touch her lower abdomen to indicate where the bladder is.

Accident Recovery

Until your child can predict his need for the potty and get himself there reliably, hold regular potty sits as described in the previous chapter. Studies show that one-third of parents fail to take their child to the potty regularly, and about a third fail to confront accidents. Both are associated with longer training times and chronic toileting problems. Keep the following in mind:

- Don't ask your child if he needs to use the potty when you are quite sure he does—send him!
- Follow the suggestions described in the previous chapter for managing tantrums.
- Set limits by teaching your child to clean up accidents, and monitor to ensure he does.
- If your child refuses to help with cleanup, have him sit down nearby so he can learn by watching.

Unless your child responds to being told to go potty by pulling down her pants and doing her business on the floor right before your very eyes as an act of clear defiance, you must assume that accidents are just that: accidents. And whether purposeful or not, the proper response is *not* to vent your dissatisfaction by engaging in the blame-and-shame game. Doing so is likely to further alienate a defiant child and will needlessly humiliate a youngster who is doing her best and really wants to please you.

All children (and adults!) make mistakes. The secret is to learn how to undo the damage. If children cannot refrain from having accidents for whatever reason, they need to learn to clean them up. Although teaching a child to mop up takes longer than doing it yourself in the short run, in the long run your child will be able to manage most of the chores on his own. Until youngsters are old enough to handle cleaning agents, carry buckets of water, and wield mops as needed to remove puddles and piles, they can participate in cleaning themselves up.

Accordingly, you might pop your child into the tub for a quick bath each time she wets and soils and help her put on clean clothes afterward. She can help carry her soiled laundry to the washer and transfer it to the dryer when it is done. By age four, your child should be able to handle these chores on her own, assuming you provide a stepping stool so she can reach the doors and show her which buttons to push. (You still need to handle chemicals and detergents yourself because they are poisons.) When the laundry is done, have your toddler carry her clean clothes to her room. Researchers Polaha, Warzak, and Dittmer-McMahon suggest that having youngsters handle cleanup can be effective when done in a nonpunitive manner.

Most youngsters think that doing the laundry is great fun for the first day or two. Frustrated parents who want their youngster to suffer over accidents as they themselves have been suffering often complain that their children enjoy these tasks. Assigning extra baths to a tot who loves to play in the tub and laundry chores to a child who is enamored with big machines may not seem like a proper punishment. The goal of potty training, however, is to teach hygiene. Once your child can clean himself up, an important goal has been accomplished.

In actuality, children soon tire of the baths and time-consuming laundry chores, so they become very motivated for potty training in short order. In the meantime they acquire laun-dry skills they can use for the rest of their lives. This puts them ahead of the pack as they make their way down the long road to independence. Whether or not you hold a victory celebration, such an accomplishment is definitely worth a party.

Potty-Training Baggage

Some three- and four-year-olds arrive at the potty-training sta-tion toting heavy loads of emotional baggage. You need to do what you can to relieve any worries that might serve to slow your child's departure. Remain alert to signs that he has picked up some undesirable souvenirs during his previous travels, as they can impede progress en route.

A common problem when potty training older children stems from previous potty-training attempts that failed. Youngsters may have concluded that potty training is overly challenging or, worse, that their personal incompetence or laziness drove their parents' decision to call a halt to the lessons. Aborted potty-training efforts can erode children's confidence: the prospect of resuming them can be a source of anxiety and dread. Obviously it is better to provide a fresh start. If your child becomes upset when you announce plans to start potty training again, it is safe

Quick Trip

If your child has had some negative potty-training experiences, do some damage control *before* starting to teach. Accept responsibility for past problems. Explain that now you have read a book on the subject and are ready to teach.

to conclude that he is harboring some worries or concerns about the process. If he suddenly falls silent, appears grim, or changes the subject when you mention potty training, it's likely that something about the potty troubles him.

It helps for your child to start with a positive attitude. Hold a frank discussion to determine your child's thoughts about and attitude toward the potty. Ask if he thinks learning to use the potty is easy or hard. Ask how his peers feel about using the potty. Ask if anything about the potty worries or scares him. Few toddlers can produce instant answers. Avoid hurrying when you broach emotionally loaded issues. Whether you have difficulties mobilizing your child's enthusiasm for the project or get stalled along the way, you need to determine what is happening. To find out what is on your child's mind, take care to avoid these common kiddy-communication pitfalls:

- **Not providing sufficient time for children to collect their thoughts and respond.** Pause for ten seconds after asking a question, and then repeat it. Do this even if your child is not talking yet so she has a chance to ponder the matter.
- **Answering for your child.** If your child isn't talking yet, you need to supply the questions and the answers. List some items that you think might be troubling her. Watch your child's reaction for clues as to which issue is significant for her. Address any areas that you believe to be of concern.
- **Belittling or discounting your child's concerns.** Treat your child's concerns as serious, and address them directly.
- **Failing to leave the door open for future discussions.** After you attempt a conversation, remain alert for out-of-the-blue comments that might signal a need for information or reassurance.

In the meantime, strive to unburden your child of old baggage by addressing past potty-training problems directly. One way to do this is to take responsibility for anything and everything that went wrong in the past:

- Explain that some parents teach little kids to use the potty, but you thought it best to wait until he was older.
- Explain that you started teaching him when he was little but decided he wasn't ready and stopped.
- Explain that when you tried potty training before, you were too busy to stick with it and take him to the potty regularly so he could learn properly.
- Explain that you didn't really know how to go about teaching him to use the potty.

The fear of having accidents makes the whole potty trip terribly worrisome for many children. If there was a lot of upset over accidents during past training attempts or your child is a dedicated rule follower, you might add that you decided it was best for her to stop training until you felt more able to cope. Reassure your youngster that learning takes time and that most children do have some accidents. Tell her that because she is older, accidents won't upset you like they did in the past. You will simply teach her how to clean them up herself.

This Is Your Captain Speaking

Many pediatricians and child psychologists warn that it is wrong for parents to pressure their youngster about using the potty. Authors say pressure from parents is disrespectful, is invasive, erodes self-esteem, and creates long-term emotional conflicts. But the very same experts advocate allowing peer pressure from preschool, kindergarten, and elementary school classmates to provide the motivation.

Quick Trip

Many children are basically being raised by their peers these days, but that is unfortunate. Your child needs *you* to be his primary teacher. You can't wait for peer pressure to motivate your child for potty training during preschool or kindergarten. By applying some positive pressure of your own, you may be able to keep your child motivated during potty training and protect him from being emotionally battered by others. Gently letting your child know that you dislike the smell of poopy diapers, and teaching him how to keep himself clean can protect him from painful experiences outside the family.

The sad truth is that peers dislike the smell of an untrained child and can be very cruel. Preschool children commonly exert pressure by taunting and shunning children who continue to wear diapers or wet and soil their underwear. Studies show that untrained youngsters over age four tend to be more socially isolated, have poorer self-esteem, and be less happy than their classmates.

Parent pressure can be even more destructive if emotional or physical pain is inflicted by humiliating children or meting out harsh punishments. But parent pressure is positive when it takes the form of setting limits to ensure children go to the potty regularly. It is positive when children are given consistent consequences for accidents. Mistakes are inevitable and accidents are bound to occur. Requiring children to participate in cleaning up afterwards need not be a punishment. While having to help clean up can motivate youngsters to try to avoid accidents, learning to help keep themselves and the household clean is an important skill.

Question and Answer

Is it better to teach my toddler to pee on the potty first, and then once that is learned, to poop on the potty? Or is it better to start with poop and then work on pee?

It is probably most beneficial to begin with pooping, since she is likely to pee at the same time. When a child is having a bowel movement, the bladder sphincter will automatically open and release any stored urine. Hence, by focusing on pooping, you teach about peeing, too.

10

Nighttime Accommodations

Bed-Wetting Solutions

At age three and a half, Billy still wasn't potty trained. His frantic parents had him create a wish list of toys, privileges, and activities, and they used it to develop a reward system. If Billy stayed dry all morning he received a reward at noon; if he stayed dry all afternoon he received a reward at dinner, and so forth. Billy got motivated and was soon staying dry all day. Nevertheless, he continued to wet the bed at night.

Billy's parents began to suspect a physical problem and took him to the doctor. They were dismayed to learn that bed-wetting was often hereditary. In fact, Billy's father had wet the bed until age seven. His parents resigned themselves to waiting for the problem to clear up on its own.

At a social gathering, Billy's mother happened to mention her continuing problems with wet sheets to a dentist friend. The friend explained that some children have an exceptionally small upper palate, a slightly misshapen jaw, or another physical problem that makes it harder for them to breathe properly when asleep. If so, their disrupted sleep patterns make it difficult for them to awaken when they need to use the potty so they wet the bed.

Billy was taken for a checkup, but the doctor found no indication that Billy suffered from sleep apnea. His mother researched the matter and learned that sleep apnea cannot *always be diagnosed when children are awake. She scheduled an appointment for an evaluation at a sleep clinic. There it was established that Billy did have sleep apnea. His smaller-than-normal upper palate prevented proper airflow when he was lying down. The recommendation was to see an orthodontist to determine if a mouth brace could correct the problem by enlarging his palate.*

When Billy learned that a solution for his bed-wetting might be on the horizon, he was overjoyed. His parents were amazed to hear him describe how much he had suffered. Apparently a classmate had correctly guessed why Billy didn't attend a sleepover and spread the news. The other children had been teasing Billy mercilessly ever since. "Maybe the kids won't be so mean after I'm fixed," Billy said. "And you'll be happier, Mom. You won't have to keep washing sheets every day!"

Billy's parents suddenly realized that they had been adding to their son's distress and humiliation. Billy was never one to show tender feelings. Often it seemed he didn't try to cooperate or care about issues that were important to them. They vowed to give him the benefit of the doubt and be more considerate when dealing with bed-wetting and other problems in the future.

Nocturnal means "night" and *enuresis* refers to involuntary wetting, so *nocturnal enuresis* is the medical term for chronic bed-wetting. Technically, nocturnal enuresis can be diagnosed when bed-wetting occurs twice per week for at least three consecutive months or causes significant distress in a child age five or older, according to the American Psychiatric Association's *Diagnostic and Statistical Manual of Mental Disorders, DSM-IV* (1994). However, less frequent wetting can still be a big problem for children as well as parents.

> **Quick Trip**
> Because daytime stress contributes to nighttime wetting, downplay accidents and contain your frustration so as not to add to your child's tension and anxiety. Instead, put your energy into shoring up your youngster's overall health and well-being. Enforce bedtimes to ensure proper rest, serve balanced meals for good nourishment, limit exposure to allergens that can irritate the bladder, and provide extra TLC.

There are two types of nocturnal enuresis: primary and secondary. Children with primary enuresis have never been consistent about staying dry at night. Those with secondary enuresis resume bed-wetting after having achieved nighttime continence. Even after staying dry at night for six months, about 25 percent of children regress at some point and go through a phase of wetting the bed.

An estimated 15 to 20 percent of five-year-olds and 10 percent of six-year-olds wet the bed. By age ten the figure drops to about 5 percent, then to 3 percent for twelve- to fourteen-year-olds. Approximately 1 to 2 percent of teens over age fifteen continue to wet.

Reluctant Travelers?

If a child resists potty training, her parents may assume that bedwetting is a motivational problem. It makes sense that youngsters might not want to rise from the comfort of the covers and head to the potty in the middle of the night. Septuagenarian Cynthia

Holmire recalls a childhood nursery rhyme that undoubtedly reflects the sentiments of many youngsters:

> Who took me from my warm, warm cot
> And set me on the cold, cold pot
> Whether I had to go or not?
> My mother!

Actually, poor motivation to get up and use the potty is at the bottom of the list of reasons children wet the bed. However, if you think that a motivational boost is necessary or that your tot needs an incentive, there are some things you can do to make middle-of-the-night potty trips easier:

- Plug in a night-light.
- Put the potty chair near your child's bed.
- Dress your child in clothing that is easy for sleepy fingers to remove.

If your tot needs to travel to another part of the house to use the potty, some additional preparation is in order:

- Leave a bathroom light on at night.
- Remove objects along the route that could cause stumbles, trips, and bumps.
- Light the path with night-lights or glow-in-the-dark adhesive strips.
- Invite your child to awaken you if she wants company.

A Johnny-Light can boost children's motivation for nighttime bathroom visits. Once this inexpensive device is installed, the toilet water emits an eerie green glow that tots find intriguing. Because the light is only visible in a completely dark room, children must go to the bathroom at night to be able to see the amazing spectacle. To order, consult Appendix B.

Some parents say that they ended bed-wetting by being firm with their youngster. They simply told their child not to wet the bed, let

Quick Trip

To overcome motivational problems, try putting your child to bed in cloth underwear instead of disposable diapers or pull-up training pants. Because disposables eliminate the sensation of wetness and hold in body heat, they lessen children's incentive to use the potty. After being awakened a few times by the unpleasant sensation of a cold, soggy bed, most youngsters decide bathroom trips are worth the trouble. If wetting continues after a week, motivation is probably not the issue.

their child know in no uncertain terms that they disliked changing the sheets, and punished accidents or offered rewards for dry sheets. However, the get-tough approach can be emotionally damaging to youngsters who are unable to control themselves. Telling them not to wet the bed is like instructing a paralyzed child to rise from her wheelchair and walk. Communicating displeasure over wet sheets and dangling presents to reward accident-free nights only serves to erode youngsters' self-esteem and makes them feel like failures.

Simple Solutions

Some simple steps can reduce or even eliminate bed-wetting:

- Reduce fluid intake late in the evening.
- Have your child go to the potty right before bedtime.
- Have your child go to the potty twice before bedtime so she empties her bladder completely—for example, right before you read a bedtime story and again just before lights-out.
- Awaken your child and take her to the potty before you go to bed and after you awaken in the morning.
- Make sure your child is not constipated.

> **Quick Trip**
>
> Do not be angry with your child for nighttime wetting. It is unlikely that he makes a conscious decision not to go to the potty or wets on purpose. Most bed wetters never wake up. Punishing and shaming them for accidents increases their stress. Stress alters their sleep patterns, making it harder for children to awaken at night. The end result is that bed-wetting worsens.

An overly full bowel puts pressure on the bladder, causing children to urinate more frequently, so it is important to address problems with constipation. Also, children may not completely void when they are half-asleep, so if you take your child to the potty at night, remind him to push. Reducing fluid intake before bedtime makes sense, but don't withhold all beverages after dinner. When children are dehydrated, their urine becomes more concentrated and the urinary urge intensifies. The need to pee develops so quickly and is so strong that children have a harder time getting to the potty in time.

Travel Glitches

After determining that motivation to keep the sheets dry is not the issue, most parents begin to wonder whether something is physically wrong with their child. In general, any condition that causes children to urinate more frequently than normal during the day is also likely to cause bed-wetting.

Two common conditions explain why nighttime wetting usually resolves as children mature. People require fewer bathroom trips at night because a hormone slows the production of urine during sleep. Some youngsters are deficient in this hormone. Medication can help them keep the sheets dry until their bodies begin producing enough hormone on their own. A second condition is small bladder size. Children with small bladders may not be able to make it through the night without a potty trip. As the bladder grows it can accommodate more urine.

Some other problems are commonly associated with bedwetting:

- **Medication side effects.** Check with your pediatrician or pharmacist to find out whether any of your child's medications increase urination.
- **Bladder infections.** Symptoms of urinary tract infections commonly include needing to urinate more often, painful urination (commonly a burning sensation), lower back pain, feeling generally unwell, cloudy urine, and fever. A round of antibiotics may be all that's needed to clear up a bladder infection, but children need immediate medical treatment to prevent kidney damage. Eradicating chronic urinary tract infections sometimes ends problems with bed-wetting.
- **Diabetes.** Symptoms of diabetes include frequent urination, excessive thirst, increased appetite, weight loss, fatigue, blurred vision, fruity-smelling breath, wounds that do not heal, itchy skin, bladder infections, and tingling feet. Contact your healthcare provider as soon as possible if your child exhibits any of these symptoms.
- **Constipation.** The increased pressure on the bladder from an overly full bowel causes children to urinate more frequently. The main cause of constipation is poor diet and lack of exercise. Instead of soda, candy, chips, and fast food, serve juice, fruit, vegetables, and whole-grain cereal and bread. Instead of letting your child watch television, encourage more vigorous physical activity. For a natural stool softener, have your child drink lots of water.

Quick Trip

About 8 percent of girls and 2 percent of boys develop a bladder infection during childhood. Girls are more at risk because the urethra is so short, making it easy for bacteria to travel to the bladder. Teach your daughter to wipe from front to back. Wiping from back to front can bring fecal matter into contact with the entrance to the urethra. Deter your little boy from bathtime experiments that involve squirting water into the penis while playing.

- **Sleep apnea.** In this condition the airway collapses during sleep. Children awaken momentarily when their oxygen supply is briefly cut off, which can happen hundreds of times a night. But because youngsters are only semiconscious, they are not aware of needing to go potty. They do not even remember awakening. Symptoms include snoring, gasping, choking, and daytime crankiness. The shape of the youngster's jaw and small upper palate can cause sleep apnea. Obesity may also be a risk factor. Have your child checked by a medical doctor. However, since it is not always possible to diagnose sleep apnea when children are awake, an evaluation at a sleep clinic may be necessary. If that is not possible, discuss the matter with an orthodontist.
- **Food sensitivities and allergies.** Caffeine functions as a diuretic, increasing urination and irritating the bladder. Check labels on beverages for caffeine and avoid serving caffeinated products to your child. Many children have problems digesting dairy products or are sensitive to certain food preservatives and dyes. Schedule an appointment with a naturopath to test for food sensitivities as well as with an allergist to assess allergies.

Unstable Bladder

The custom in recent years has been to blame parents for children's potty problems. T. Berry Brazelton asserts that early potty training increases the likelihood of bed-wetting. Actually, research does not confirm this. Studies suggest that if children are potty trained between ages eighteen and twenty-four months, they are less likely to wet the bed. Problems with bed-wetting are more common among children who are potty trained after twenty-four months old. No solid research is available to suggest how potty-trained infants and babies fare, but clinical reports suggest that bed-wetting may be rare among these groups.

Since late potty training has become the norm, the incidence of bed-wetting has increased dramatically. In 1957, Sears and his coauthors reported in *Patterns of Child Rearing* that at least 66 percent of the children they studied had stopped wetting the bed by age three. The actual figure may have been higher, since 8 percent of the parents that were interviewed couldn't remember when their youngsters' bed-wetting had ceased. In 2001, a study found that only 47 percent had stopped bed-wetting by age three. Several studies have found that children who are trained late tend to have to pee more frequently and continue to have more accidents during the day at age eleven. Frequent urination and daytime accidents are both associated with bed-wetting.

Unstable bladder, a medical condition that has become more common in recent years, is associated with starting potty training late. The main symptoms are continued bed-wetting and daytime accidents due to improper functioning of the bladder. The detrusor muscle may not remain contracted when children urinate, which keeps the bladder from emptying completely. Or the muscle may contract at unpredictable times, causing the urge to urinate to arise so quickly that children cannot get to the potty in time.

There are a number of treatments for an unstable bladder:

- Bladder retraining
- Biofeedback
- Hypnosis
- Medication
- Surgery

Take your child to a pediatric urologist if you suspect unstable bladder. If your child has this condition, you may be able to treat it by working with him at home. One method involves taking the youngster to the potty as often as is required to remain dry. This could mean a trek to the bathroom every twenty or thirty minutes. The time between potty trips is increased very gradually by adding five or ten minutes every few days until the time between potty trips is more normal. When the child urinates, he is encouraged to try to stop the flow midstream and then resume peeing. When he finishes, he is told to push to try to empty the bladder completely. The goal is to exercise and strengthen the bladder muscles until the youngster can start and stop the flow of urine at will.

Quick Trip

Storing urine in the bladder for long periods can cause bladder infections. Chronic bladder infections are associated with bed-wetting. It appears that children may not empty the bladder completely until they undergo potty training. Start training early and teach your child to push to be sure that the bladder is empty before getting off the potty. Sometimes children don't realize when they need to use the potty. If you think your child needs to use it but won't go, give her the option of sitting on the potty for one minute or sitting in time-out for two minutes.

A Visit to Dreamland

Your infant may have awakened during the first few months of life when he needed to pee. If you didn't respond until after he wet, he probably learned to ignore the rising pressure in his bladder and got good at sleeping through the night. After doing this for several years, he may be unable to awaken when his bladder is full.

Wetting most often occurs during a particular sleep stage known as non-REM sleep. During this period of especially deep sleep, children do not dream and are very hard to wake up. For most bed wetters, the challenge is teaching the brain to respond to the bladder's call by rousing the child from her slumber so she can go potty.

Try putting your child to bed in regular underwear instead of diapers. Plant the suggestion that she wake up when she needs to use the potty as you deliver your good-night kiss. The unfamiliar sensation of wearing underwear may penetrate her awareness even as she sleeps, causing her to awaken when she needs the potty. If not, there is a chance the spreading dampness will awaken her when she wets. Barring that, she will probably awaken soon after—when the urine cools and she begins to shiver. After awakening regularly for a week, her sleeping brain may start responding before the bladder overfills and waste is expelled by reflex.

If wearing underwear to bed doesn't work, try to discern your youngster's wetting pattern. Take him to the potty yourself ten to fifteen minutes before the expected flood. If you can manage to awaken him consistently before he wets for a couple of weeks, he may start awakening on his own. Unfortunately, discerning when your child wets is no small task. You may need to check the diaper every thirty minutes for several nights in a row. Most children only wet once or twice a night at predictable times, but some wet many times each night and have no pattern. A moisture-activated

> **Quick Trip**
>
> Many companies sell bed-wetting alarms and consulting services to desperate parents for outrageously inflated prices. The alarms can be purchased at discount and department stores for around seventy-five dollars. They come with detailed instruction booklets. If your child needs additional help, contact a child guidance counselor or see Appendix B for recommendations.

device designed for bed wetters can help you determine when accidents are occurring. These potty-training devices sound an alarm when a child wets.

Children over age seven can use a bed-wetting alarm to try to train themselves to awaken so they can use the toilet. The sensors are encased in a pad that lies on the bed. When a sensor detects moisture, a noisy alarm crashes through the child's sleep with enough force that the sphincter muscle snaps shut, stopping the flow of urine. Then the child can get up and use the bathroom. Over time, the brain may begin rousing her before the dreaded racket interrupts her visit to the sandman. This method is not easy. To succeed, youngsters must be very dedicated and determined. Many later relapse but quickly regain control by using the alarm for a few nights.

Medical Treatments

Several medications can speed the quest for dry sheets. One type helps children with insufficient hormone levels by reducing the amount of urine they produce at night. For children with an unstable bladder, medication can regulate bladder contractions, thereby reducing accidents. Tofranil, one of the few antidepressant medications approved for use by children, normalizes sleep patterns so that youngsters awaken more easily. Nevertheless, Tofranil has unpleasant and potentially dangerous side effects; consider carefully before going that route. Your child's physician can provide an overview of the common side effects, and a pharmacist can provide detailed information.

Acupressure, a type of massage that involves applying pressure to specific points on the lower abdomen, has been found to be an effective treatment for bed-wetting. A 2003 study reported in the *Journal of International Medical Research* compared acupressure and oxybutynin, a medication that helps calm bladder contractions. The researchers taught parents to administer acupressure to their children. After six months, 83 percent of the children receiving acupressure obtained complete or partial relief from bed-wetting, compared to only 58 percent of the children receiving medication. The researchers concluded that "nocturnal enuresis can be partially treated by oxybutynin but acupressure could be an alternative non-drug therapy. Acupressure has the advantages of being non-invasive, painless and cost-effective."

Deluxe Accommodations

In most cases, Father Time provides the one sure cure for bed-wetting. About 99 percent of youngsters simply outgrow the condition. Bed-wetting ends for children with especially small bladders when they grow enough to hold normal quantities of urine. Brain waves change as the brain and central nervous system mature, altering sleep patterns so youngsters can awaken more easily. Until then, the only option may be to find ways to keep your youngster comfortable at night, the bed sanitary, and your own workload to a minimum.

Coping with bed-wetting is no small task. It is a given that you will at times feel frustrated and resentful about the mounds of bedding and problematic odor. The question is how you handle your emotions. Chastising your tot will likely add to his upset without solving the problem. Although your youngster may not seem to mind wetting the bed, research suggests that bed wetters do suffer psychologically. If youngsters awaken after accidents, the quality of their sleep can be affected, especially if they wet several times each night.

As bed wetters add candles to their birthday cakes, the fallout from bed-wetting tends to get worse. Most children feel compelled to decline invitations to sleep over at friends' houses. Bed wetters typically avoid camping trips, slumber parties, and summer camp. The social stigma can be intense, and many youngsters are haunted by the possibility of having their peers discover their shameful secret. Siblings taunt and even blackmail children with this problem, threatening to expose them.

Even bed wetters with compassionate, understanding parents may feel guilty about the extra workload their problem creates. Don't be surprised if you find damp sheets tucked in the back of a closet and moldering pajamas hidden under the bed. The obvi-

Quick Trip

To help your bed wetter get a good night's sleep, lay out a clean pair of pajamas and a sleeping bag at bedtime. This way, your child can quickly change into dry clothes and snuggle in. Save sheet-changing and laundry chores until morning. For help locating sleeping bag liners, mattress pads, vinyl sheets, alarms, and other bed-wetting lifesavers, see Appendix B.

ous solution is to remain upbeat and cheerful as you have your youngster assist when you change sheets. Then, if wetting continues, she will eventually be able to manage the cleanup chores herself. As long as you handle dangerous cleaning agents yourself, everyone benefits when children learn how to strip a bed, put on clean sheets, and run a load of laundry. Doing so accomplishes the following:

- Boosts motivation to eliminate bed-wetting
- Promotes independence
- Relieves children's guilt
- Helps children feel more in control
- Lessens parents' workload
- Reduces parents' resentment

An Arduous Journey

Elementary school students who wet the bed tend to have more behavioral, social, speech, and learning problems. Their adjustment and academic problems commonly worsen as they progress toward high school. Your child needs all the help you can give him. Do what you can to improve his lifestyle:

- Cut out the junk food.
- Eliminate television and video games on school nights.
- Be strict about bedtime to help ensure proper rest.
- Insist on daily exercise.

Depressed children spend more time in the non-REM deep-sleep cycle, which is when most bed-wetting occurs. This may explain why being more stressed or tired than usual can trigger a bout of bed-wetting or increase the number of incidents on some night. Strive to make your home especially kid-friendly. To do this, avoid nagging and find workable solutions to problems. Set limits to help your child develop self-discipline. Spend time enjoying one another by talking or playing each day. Enroll in a parenting course and take your child for counseling sooner rather than later if problems develop at home, school, or in the neighborhood. Do your best to make your youngster's journey through childhood as healthy and happy as possible.

Question and Answer

My son no longer wets the bed, but he continues to wake me up to take him to the potty. I leave the bathroom light on, and he can handle the potty without help. How can I get him to go by himself?

Sometimes rewards can help. Wrap a small gift and put it in the bathroom—out of reach but positioned so your son can see it. When he awakens you in the middle of the night, remind him that if he can go to the potty by himself, you will give him his present in the morning.

Appendix A

Emergency Landings—
Solving Special Problems

My toddler is almost two years old. I am convinced he knows when he needs to use the potty, but he puts off going and has accidents. What can I do?

Children often misjudge how long they can postpone a potty trip and how long it will take them to arrive once they head in that direction. A technique used by Nathan Azrin and Richard Foxx described in *Toilet Training in Less than a Day* can help youngsters age twenty-one months and older.

Whenever your child has an accident, immediately take him to the spot where it happened and say, "You are supposed to pee in the potty, not in your diaper. You need to practice going potty!" Hurry your child to the potty, tell him to remove his pants, have him sit down for one to two seconds, then tell him to stand up, pull up his pants, and return to where the accident occurred. Then say, "You're supposed to pee in the potty! You need more practice going to the potty!" Repeat the entire procedure five or six times before changing your child into clean clothes.

Toddlers predictably become upset during these forced practice sessions. Many balk and have tantrums. Parents are supposed to ignore tantrums and physically guide or carry an uncooperative youngster to the potty, remove her pants for her, sit her on the potty for a second or two, put her pants back on, and return her to the scene of the accident. Parents are to do this again and again while remaining calm and using as little physical force as possible to keep their youngster on track. Yelling at uncooperative tots just makes them more upset and resistant while distracting them from the task at hand.

This method can be very stressful. Some parents cannot contain themselves when struggling with a child who is screaming and resisting. Parents must end a practice session immediately if they feel inclined to lash out. This technique is very effective if parents can remain calm, but many cannot. Some parents consider this technique too severe and overly upsetting for their child.

My child was almost completely trained. Suddenly she started refusing to use the potty and had so many accidents that I had to put her back in diapers. She gets upset if I even mention the potty. What could the problem be?

Children can regress for any number of reasons. However, at the first sign of any unexplained toileting problem, constipation should be considered as a possible culprit. It is the leading cause of sudden potty refusals. Technically defined as having fewer than three bowel movements per week, constipation can be a problem for children who have more frequent movements, according to an article in the *American Family Physician*. Signs of constipation include pain, crying, excessive straining during bowel movements, and holding back stool. An infant who has only one bowel movement per day or a young child who has fewer than one stool every two days should be checked by a pediatrician even if there are no obvious signs of discomfort.

Hard stool need not be a problem if it is small enough to pass through the rectum without causing discomfort. Hard, wide stool, on the other hand, stretches the rectum, which is painful.

If you find a bit of blood in your child's poop, the rectum may have actually been torn during a difficult bowel movement.

Over three-quarters of two-year-olds who have problems are constipated. The problem usually stems from poor diet, insufficient water intake, and inadequate exercise. The effects of constipation on potty training tend to be profound. One study found that 55 percent of children with toileting problems were constipated. Difficult-to-train tots were significantly more likely to be constipated and to have problems such as hiding dirty underwear and refusing to use the potty for bowel movements.

Besides causing pain, an overly full bowel puts pressure on the bladder, causing youngsters to need to urinate more frequently. This can increase the number of wetting accidents. When pushing to urinate, additional pressure is placed on the bowel, which can trigger uncomfortable cramps. Little ones don't understand what is going on; all they know is that they hurt when they try to use the potty to pee as well as to poop. It is understandable that they act as if the potty were some sort of torture chamber. Constipation should be dealt with immediately.

My son was completely trained, but then he started pooping in his pants and lying about it. This is unlike him, as he is generally well behaved. I don't know what to make of the problem or how to solve it.

It is possible that your son has encopresis, a serious condition that develops when stool becomes impacted. In this condition, a mass that is too large and hard to pass collects inside the bowel. Water, a natural stool softener, cannot penetrate the stool. Instead, water leaks around the mass and out of the rectum.

In a typical case, the rectum has been stretched and torn from previous efforts to pass hard bowel movements, leaving the muscles weakened and numb. Initially, children are in great pain, but they eventually lose all sensation. At that point they are unaware they are passing small amounts of soft stool. Usually the stool is watery, but it can sometimes appear like an especially soft bowel movement.

Parents see their child's soiled underwear and commonly assume he simply failed to use the potty. When they confront him and he denies having had an accident despite the "evidence," they assume he is lying. As family tensions heat up, many youngsters are subjected to increasingly severe punishments as their frustrated parents struggle to convince their children that they must not go potty in their pants. Meanwhile, the noxious odor causes older children to be shunned by peers. Encopresis is associated with serious emotional problems, but not in the way psychologists once thought. Long believed to be caused by emotional problems, it is now understood that encopresis causes emotional problems rather than being the result of them.

Correcting encopresis usually requires a six-month treatment regime as follows:

1. Soften the mass of hard stool so the child can pass it.
2. Allow time for the rectum to heal and the muscles to regain their elasticity.
3. Help the child overcome the emotional trauma.

A laxative treatment is usually required to soften hard stool. A daily dose of mineral oil is often used. It can be mixed into juice or added to salads. Because mineral oil interferes with vitamin absorption, a supplement is commonly required. Check with your health-care provider before administering mineral oil to your child.

Send your son to the bathroom each day for a fifteen-minute potty sit. Continue to monitor your child's movements, and look for very watery or slightly bloody stool. Tell an older child to let you know immediately if he is even slightly constipated. Ever after the problem is finally corrected, the risk of relapse is very high.

Ever since my daughter was an infant, she has had problems with constipation. The doctor never seemed to consider it a serious problem, but she would scream in pain when she pooped. Meanwhile, my other daughter often has bouts of diarrhea for no apparent reason. What can I do to help them?

A number of popular foods can cause constipation:

- Milk and milk products, such as cheese and ice cream
- Chocolate
- Peanuts and peanut butter
- Bananas
- Gelatin
- Apples

Some of these foods, however, can also cause exceptionally loose stool, usually due to food allergies and chemical sensitivities. The following foods and food additives commonly trigger allergic reactions:

- Milk
- Wheat
- Rye
- Barley
- Oats
- Eggs
- Soy
- Corn
- Citrus fruits
- Nuts

- Chocolate
- Coffee
- Artificial colorings
- Artificial flavors
- Preservatives

Every child's system is different, so vary your children's diets to see which foods are causing problems. For example, although bananas and apples cause some youngsters to become terribly constipated, these fruits cause diarrhea in others.

In general, the first line of treatment for constipation is a change in diet. Pediatrician and author William Sears recommends adding two to three daily glasses of Mother Nature's stool softener—water—to your child's diet. Eliminate processed foods and provide more whole grains, fresh fruits, and fresh vegetables to add fiber to her diet. Fiber promotes regularity.

For more intensive laxative treatment, daily doses of diluted prune juice containing pulp tend to be especially effective. Sears recommends one or two tablespoons for a six-month-old baby to eight ounces for a toddler. If your child dislikes the taste, prune juice can be mixed with a food he likes. Other options include apricots, pears, plums, and peaches.

Another option Sears recommends is one teaspoon a day of flax oil for infants, two teaspoons a day for toddlers. This healthy choice contains omega-3 fatty acids and can be stirred into juice, poured over salad dressing, or spread onto a peanut butter sandwich. Flaxseed meal is another option. It has the added benefit of containing fiber. Try mixing one tablespoon each day into your child's cereal. Psyllium husks, available at health food stores, can also be effective. Psyllium is sold over the counter as Metamucil. Psyllium is highly effective if taken with eight ounces of water. Taken dry, however, it can worsen constipation. The starting dose for a toddler is one teaspoon per day, which can be increased to two teaspoons per day if needed. See askdrsears.com for more information on treatments for constipation.

Phyllis Braun, a licensed massage therapist, recommends an ancient folk remedy for relieving constipation. The remedy involves drawing "magic circles" on your child's lower abdomen. Begin by placing your fingertips just below your child's navel. Apply steady, gentle but firm pressure as you slowly move your hand clockwise, creating successively larger circles. The largest circle should extend from the lower stomach to just above the pubic bone. The process should take about twenty seconds. Repeat once or twice a day for several days.

It's hard to know why magic circles work. Does the pressure trigger the muscles of the bowel to contract to start a movement? Does the minimassage relax your child so she can open the anal sphincter muscle and pass stool? Whatever the reason, look for relief in twenty-four hours in the form of a softer bowel movement.

My daughter used to be afraid of public restrooms. Now when we go shopping she keeps saying she needs to pee, but when I take her she can't use the toilet. What's going on?

The loud, noisy toilets commonly found in public restrooms tend to be very frightening to young children. But once they overcome their fear, youngsters are fascinated by the toilets, stalls, sinks, hand dryers, soap, and towels. Exploring foreign potty lands is, from a child's point of view, one of the few rewards for all of the work they devote to potty training. Try to be patient while your daughter satisfies her curiosity. Knowing your child's patterns can help you make better guesses about whether she wants to see a public toilet or use one.

My son won't sit on his potty seat to poo. He hides behind the couch or in his bedroom closet when he needs to do his business. How can I get him to use the potty?

Many toddlers have had a bad experience pooping in the toilet while sitting on a potty seat. Being so high off the ground can unnerve them. If they are a bit constipated, a splash of cold water when passing hard stool can frighten them. Afterward, they avoid pooping in the potty. Also, because they lack support for their feet while sitting so high off the ground, they cannot get enough leverage to push. That makes it more difficult for them to pass movements. The first step is to get your child a potty chair. He will feel more secure closer to the ground and can rest his feet on the floor to get proper leverage. There is no risk that he will be frightened by a sudden splash of cold water.

Many older youngsters hide when having bowel movements because they are trying to protect their precious possessions from being flushed away. If you can get your youngster to poop in the toilet, don't flush the toilet until he has left the room.

Older toddlers may have become accustomed to standing during bowel movements over several years. They have difficulty working their muscles when sitting and can't readily relieve themselves. As a consequence, they resist using the potty when pooping but don't mind peeing into it. If your child insists on using a diaper and is accustomed to standing to eliminate, try laying a clean diaper on the bathroom floor and help him straddle it when he needs to poop. That way, he will become accustomed to having bowel movements in the bathroom, can eliminate bare bottomed, and won't make such a mess. After he becomes comfortable with this position and environment, it will be a smaller step to eliminating into the potty.

Alternatively, let him wear a diaper while he sits on the potty chair to poop. When he is comfortable with this, lay the diaper across the potty bowl when he needs to eliminate. Next, cut a small hole in the diaper and lay it across the potty bowl. Each day thereafter provide a diaper with a slightly larger hole.

Some toddlers hide when pooping because they have been teased and are ashamed to be seen. Two books can help children overcome shame and develop a healthier attitude toward elimination. *Everyone Poops (My Body Science)* by Taro Gomi and Amanda Mayer Stinchecum has helped many youngsters accept the process as natural. You may need to prepare yourself for the graphic cartoon elephants and their giant brown piles, but children are not offended. *Where's the Poop?* by Julie Markes and Susan Kathleen Hartung is a lift-the-flap book. It teaches that every creature has a different place to poop—and for children, the place is the potty.

My child was happy to use the potty until the novelty wore off. Now I can't get him to use it. What do you suggest?

You can try a variety of things:

- Tint the toilet bowl water with blue food dye. Your child will enjoy watching it turn green when he urinates.
- Buy your son a fireman's hat. Announce that there is a fire in the toilet when you think he needs to pee, and send him to sprinkle the imaginary blaze.
- Drop a Ping-Pong ball into the toilet bowl, and suggest he try to hit the target.
- Explain that pee and poop are sad because they want to go home. To get there, your son has to put them in the toilet and start the engine to send them on their way by flushing so they can travel through the pipes to where they live. Suggest that your son give them a proper send-off by waving bye-bye as he flushes.

- Play the Mama-is-going-to-tickle-you game. Send your child scurrying toward the bathroom by threatening to tickle him if you catch him before he gets onto the potty. Make sure to give him a few little tickles when he arrives so he'll love the game and want to play again. Be careful, though. So much laughter can cause your child to have an accident before he makes it to the potty.
- Accompany your child to the bathroom to make the time more pleasant. Many parents encourage their children to go by themselves before they are ready for so much independence.

My eighteen-month-old girl will sit on the potty for a long time but nothing happens until I give up and let her off to go play. I really think she wants to cooperate, but sometimes I'm not so sure if she has accidents just to spite me.

It is common for children to have an accident soon after an unsuccessful attempt to use the potty. When children are too tense, they cannot release waste. When they relax, their sphincter muscles also relax.

Do *not* assume your toddler is being defiant by having an accident as soon as her diaper is back on after a long potty sit. By keeping her in diapers to prevent messy accidents, you probably conditioned her sphincters to remain closed whenever her bottom is bare.

To reverse sphincter conditioning, have your daughter go bare bottomed for several days. Little girls can wear a dress but not underwear. The typical pattern is for the sphincters to remain closed for a long time—some youngsters have gone twelve hours without urinating. But eventually the pressure becomes too great and waste is expelled by reflex. After an accident or two, children are usually able to open the sphincters without needing to be covered in a diaper.

Appendix B

Resources

Books

Azrin, Nathan H., and Richard M. Foxx. *Toilet Training in Less than a Day*. New York City: Simon & Schuster, 1974. This extremely strict, somewhat controversial method can be effective for children over age twenty-one months. For youngsters to maintain their gains, parents must continue to attend to accidents.

Bakker, Wilhelmina. *Research into the Influence of Potty-Training on Lower Urinary Tract Dysfunction*. Antwerp, Belgium: University of Antwerp, 2002. This doctoral thesis summarizes most of the important toilet-training research investigations.

Bauer, Ingrid. *Diaper Free! The Gentle Wisdom of Natural Infant Hygiene*. Saltspring Island, British Columbia: Natural Wisdom Press, 2001. The author shares her personal experiences and gives research-based advice on infant potty training.

Boucke, Laurie. *Infant Potty Training: A Gentle and Primeval Method Adapted to Modern Living*. Lafayette, CO: White-Boucke Publishing, Inc., 2000. This comprehensive resource contains detailed guidelines, photos, testimonials, along with summaries of medical research and cross-cultural research studies.

Boucke, Laurie. *Infant Potty Basics: With or Without Diapers, the Natural Way*. Lafayette, CO: White-Boucke Publishing, Inc., 2003. Learn the gentle art of infant pottying, with or without diapers.

Foxx, Richard M., and Nathan H. Azrin. *Toilet Training the Retarded: A Rapid Program for Day and Nighttime Independent Toileting.* Champaign, IL: Research Press, 1973. This program became the model for the toddler training method presented in *Toilet Training in Less than a Day.*

Herbert, Martin. *Toilet Training, Bedwetting, and Soiling.* London: The British Psychological Society, 1996. Dr. Herbert presents facts and information for training older toddlers.

Lansky, Vicki. *Toilet Training: A Practical Guide to Daytime and Nighttime Training.* Minnetonka, MN: Book Peddlers, 2002. This popular book describes the "no-pressure" approach for toilet training older toddlers and preschoolers.

Mack, Alison, and David Wilensky. *Dry All Night: The Picture Book Technique That Stops Bedwetting.* New York City: Little Brown & Company, 1990. Part 1 is for parents; Part 2 is for kids. Lots of happy readers say this book helped their youngsters after other methods failed.

Maizels, Max, Diane Rosenbaum, and Barbara Keating. *Getting to Dry: How to Help Your Child Overcome Bedwetting.* Boston: Harvard Common Press, 1999. This comprehensive book provides a wealth of information about the causes of and treatments for bed-wetting.

Pillari-Penner, Karen. *It's Time! A Potty Training Guide.* iUniverse, Inc., 2004. This intensive, no-nonsense method is designed to get older toddlers potty trained in a month. It is too harsh for sensitive youngsters but may help children who benefit from strict limits.

Schaefer, Charles E., and Theresa Foy DiGeronimo. *Toilet Training Without Tears.* New York City: Penguin Group, 1997. The authors include information on training infants, babies, and toddlers as well as developmentally delayed and physically handicapped children.

Van Pelt, Katie. *Potty Training Your Baby*. New York City: Signet, 2002. This book provides detailed instructions on how to potty train your baby.

Videos and DVDs

Once Upon a Potty for Him; Once Upon a Potty for Her (DVD). Barron's Educational Series, Inc., 1990. Your child may be more motivated after seeing other little ones use the potty and learning the potty song.
The Potty Project: A Revolutionary Concept to Toilet Train Your Baby (VHS). Penton Overseas, Inc, 2001. See demonstrations of infant potty training narrated by a pediatrician.

Potty-Training Aids

Anatomically correct dolls that wet. The Acquini potty-training doll is machine washable. It is extremely useful because it comes with a miniature baby bottle, a potty, and an instruction book containing potty-training tips. Using a doll that wets is a good way to demonstrate the steps in using the potty for older toddlers. Visit pottytrainingconcepts.com to order.
Bed-wetting aids. For sleeping bag liners, mattress pads, vinyl sheets, alarms, and other bed-wetting lifesavers, visit bedwettingstore.com.
Infant potty-training advice and support. Join an e-mail discussion list at
http://groups.yahoo.com/group/eliminationcommunication,
http://groups.yahoo.com/group/naturalinfanthygiene, or

http://groups.yahoo.com/group/earlytoileting. Post questions to the message board at http://messageboards.ivillage.com/iv -ppelimtrain?redircnt=2 or through the discussion forum at mothering.com/discussions/forumdisplay.php?s=&forumid=227.

Natural diapering products. Weebees.com has an extensive line of diapers, wraps, and covers with instructions for folding, pinning, and laundering.

Potty light. Install the Johnny-Light to give your child an incentive to get out of bed at night to use the potty. Order from http://inventionshowcase.com or call (888) 566-5483.

Potty-training charts and certificates. Use these motivational aids to track your child's progress and to reward successes. Download free from drsonna.org and print at home.

Potty-training clothing for toddlers. Pants with open crotches sewn by moms working from home can be purchased at charlottescloset.com.

Potty-training help line. E-mail your potty-training problems and questions to the author and receive a personalized reply within forty-eight hours, or schedule a telephone consultation. Visit drsonna.org.

Relaxation aid. Teach your child to relax by reading the storybook *I Take a DEEEP Breath* by Sharon Penchina and Stuart Hoffman (Arizona: 2 Imagine Publishing, 2005) to your child during potty sits.

Endnotes

Chapter 1

American Academy of Pediatrics toilet-training readiness Web page, aap.org/healthtopics/toilettraining.cfm. Accessed November 2004.

Anderson, R. C., and J. H. Anderson. "Acute Respiratory Effects of Diaper Emissions." *Archive of Environmental Health* 54 (1999): 353–58.

Blum, Nathan J., Bruce Taubaum, and Nicole Nemeth. "Relationship Between Age at Initiation of Toilet Training and Duration of Training: A Prospective Study." *Pediatrics* 111 (2003): 810–14.

Boucke, Laurie. *Infant Potty Training: A Gentle and Primeval Method Adapted to Modern Living*. Lafayette, CO: White-Boucke Publishing, Inc., 2000.

Boyle, Matthew. "Dueling Diapers: Think Big Companies Can't Innovate? Look How Kimberly-Clark and P&G are Fighting over Disposable Training Pants." *Fortune* 147 (2003): 115.

Brazelton, T. Berry. "A Child-Oriented Approach to Toilet Training." *Pediatrics* 29 (1962): 121–28.

Dyer, Davis, Frederick Dalzell, and Rowena Olegario. *Rising Tide: Lessons from 165 Years of Brand Building at Procter & Gamble*. Boston: Harvard Business School Press, 2004.

Karlberg, Ann-Therese, and Kerstin Magnusson. "Rosin Components Identified in Diapers." *Contact Dermatitis* 34 (1996): 176–80.

Kawauchi, Akihiro, Yoshiyuki Tanaka, Yutaka Yamao, Mitsuhiko Inaba, Motohiro Kanazawa, Osamu Ukimura, Yoichi Mizutani, and Tsuneharu Miki. "Follow-Up Study of Bedwetting from 3 to 5 Years of Age." *Pediatric Urology* 58 (2001): 772–76.

Lemonick, Michael D. "War of the Diapers: A Parenting Guru Claims We've Been Doing Potty Training All Wrong." *Time* 153 (1999): 64.

Luxem, Michael, and E. Christophersen. "Behavioral Toilet Training in Early Childhood: Research, Practice, and Implications." *Journal of Developmental Behavioral Pediatrics* 15 (1994): 370–78.

National Association of Diaper Services Web page, diapernet .com. Accessed December 2004.

Neff, Jack. "Kids Take Longer to Train; Diaper Business Swells." *Advertising Age* 69 (1998): 3.

Partsch, C. J., M. Aukamp, and W. G. Sippell. "Scrotal Temperature Is Increased in Disposable Plastic Lined Nappies." *Archives of Disease in Childhood* 83 (2000): 364–68.

Pediatric History Center. *T. Berry Brazelton Oral History Project.* Elk Grove Village, IL: American Academy of Pediatrics, 1997.

Polaha, Jodi, William J.Warzak, and Karen Dittmer-McMahon. "Toilet Training in Primary Care: Current Practice and Recommendations from Behavioral Pediatrics." *Journal of Developmental & Behavioral Pediatrics* 23 (December 2002): 424–29.

Schonwald, Alison, Lon Sherritt, Ann Stadtler, and Carolyn Bridgemohan. "Factors Associated with Difficult Toilet Training." *Pediatrics* 113 (2004): 1753–57.

Schum, Timothy R., T. M. Kolb, T. L. McAuliffe, M. D. Simms, R. L. Underhill, and M. Lewis. "Sequential Acquisition of Toilet-Training Skills: A Descriptive Study of Gender and Age Differences in Normal Children." *Pediatrics* 109 (2002): 48.

Schum, Timothy R., T. L. McAuliffe, M. D. Simms, J. A. Walter, M. Lewis, and R. Pupp. "Factors Associated with Toilet

Training in the 1990s." *Ambulatory Pediatrics* 1 (2001): 79–86.

Sears, Robert R., Eleanor E. Maccoby, and Harry Levin. *Patterns of Child Rearing*. New York City: Row, Peterson & Company, 1957.

Spock, Benjamin. *The Pocket Book of Baby and Child Care*. New York City: Pocket Books, Inc., 1946.

Watson, John. *Psychological Care of Infant and Child*. New York City: W. W. Norton & Company, Inc., 1928.

Weiss and Associates Marketing Research. A diaper rash survey among diaper service customers. dy-dee.com. Accessed January 2005.

Wolraich, Mark L. *American Academy of Pediatrics Guide to Toilet Training*. New York City: Bantam Books, 2003.

Chapter 2

American Academy of Pediatrics toilet-training readiness Web page, aap.org/healthtopics/toilettraining.cfm. Accessed December 2004.

Bakker, Wilhelmina. *Research into the Influence of Potty-Training on Lower Urinary Tract Dysfunction*. Antwerp, Belgium: University of Antwerp, 2002.

Brazelton, T. Berry. *Touchpoints: The Essential Reference*. Reading, MA: Addison-Wesley Publishing Co., 1992.

Faull, Jan. *Mommy I Have to Go Potty!* Seattle: Parenting Press, Inc., 1996.

Jones, Michael Owen. "What's Disgusting, Why, and What Does It Matter?" *Journal of Folklore Research* 37 (January–April 2000): 53–71.

Kawauchi, Akihiro, Yoshiyuki Tanaka, Yutaka Yamao, Mitsuhiko Inaba, Motohiro Kanazawa, Osamu Ukimura, Yoichi Mizutani, and Tsuneharu Miki. "Follow-Up Study of Bedwetting from 3 to 5 Years of Age." *Pediatric Urology* 58 (2001): 772–76.

Kemp, Mario K. *Preventing Toddler Self Wetting: A Study of Three Methods*. St. Joseph, MO: Department of Psychology, Missouri Western State College, 2004.

Maizels, Max, Kevin Gandhy, Barbara Keating, and Diane Rosenbaum. "Diagnosis and Treatment for Children Who Cannot Control Urination." *Current Problems in Pediatrics* 10 (1993): 402–50.

Mash, Eric J., and Russell A. Barkley. *Child Psychopathology*. New York City: Guilford Press, 1996.

Monte, Christopher. *Beneath the Mask: An Introduction to Theories of Personality*, Sixth Edition. Dallas: Harcourt-Brace College Publishers, 1999.

Reiff, Michael I. "Toilet Training." *Journal of Developmental & Behavioral Pediatrics* 25 (2004): 140.

Schmitt, Barton D. "Toilet Training Problems: Underachievers, Refusers, and Stool Holders." *Contemporary Pediatrics* 21, no. 4 (April 2004): 71–82.

Sigelman, Carol K., and David R. Shaffer. *Life-Span Human Development*, Second Edition. Belmont, CA: Brooks/Cole Publishing Company, 1995.

Watson, John. *Psychological Care of Infant and Child*. New York City: W. W. Norton & Company, Inc., 1928.

Chapter 3

Boucke, Laurie. *Infant Potty Basics: With or Without Diapers, the Natural Way*. Lafayette, CO: White-Boucke Publishing, Inc., 2003.

deVries, Marten W., and M. Rachel deVries. "Cultural Relativity of Toilet Training Readiness: A Perspective from East Africa." *Pediatrics* 60 (1977): 170–77.

Herbert, Martin. *Toilet Training, Bedwetting, and Soiling.* London: The British Psychological Society, 1996.

Kawauchi, Akihiro, Yoshiyuki Tanaka, Yutaka Yamao, Mitsuhiko Inaba, Motohiro Kanazawa, Osamu Ukimura, Yoichi Mizutani, and Tsuneharu Miki. "Follow-Up Study of Bedwetting from 3 to 5 Years of Age." *Pediatric Urology* 58 (2001): 772–76.

Schum, Timothy R., T. L. McAuliffe, M. D. Simms, J. A. Walter, M. Lewis, and R. Pupp. "Factors Associated with Toilet Training in the 1990s." *Ambulatory Pediatrics* 1 (2001): 79–86.

Chapter 4

Bakker, E., J. D. Van Gool, M. Van Sprundet, C. Van der Auwera, and J. J. Wyndaele. "Results of a Questionnaire Evaluating the Effects of Different Methods of Toilet Training on Achieving Bladder Control." *BJU International* 90 (2002): 456–61.

Bakker, Wilhelmina. *Research into the Influence of Potty-Training on Lower Urinary Tract Dysfunction.* Antwerp, Belgium: University of Antwerp, 2002.

Bauer, Ingrid. *Diaper Free! The Gentle Wisdom of Natural Infant Hygiene.* Saltspring Island, British Columbia: Natural Wisdom Press, 2001.

Center for Disease Control. *Escherichia coli* O157:H7, cdc.gov/nci dod/dbmd/diseaseinfo/escherichiacoli_g.htm. Accessed December 2004.

Hijazy, Mahmoud. *Principles of Pediatric Dermatology*, 2000, drmhijazy.com/english/ebook.htm. Accessed January 2005.

Sears, Robert R., Eleanor E. Maccoby, and Harry Levin. *Patterns of Child Rearing.* New York City: Row, Peterson & Company, 1957.

Chapter 5

Bakker, E., J. D. Van Gool, M. Van Sprundet, C. Van der Auwera, and J. J. Wyndaele. "Results of a Questionnaire Evaluating the Effects of Different Methods of Toilet Training on Achieving Bladder Control." *BJU International* 90 (2002): 456–61.

Bakker, E., and J. J. Wyndaele. "Changes in the Toilet Training of Children During the Last 60 Years: The Cause of an Increase in Lower Urinary Tract Dysfunction?" *British Journal of Urology* 86 (2000): 248–52.

Bakker, Wilhelmina. *Research into the Influence of Potty-Training on Lower Urinary Tract Dysfunction.* Antwerp, Belgium: University of Antwerp, 2002.

Bauer, Ingrid. *Diaper Free! The Gentle Wisdom of Natural Infant Hygiene.* Saltspring Island, British Columbia, Canada: Natural Wisdom Press, 2001.

Blum, Nathan J., Bruce Taubaum, and Nicole Nemeth. "Relationship Between Age at Initiation of Toilet Training and Duration of Training: A Prospective Study." *Pediatrics* 111 (2003): 810–14.

Boucke, Laurie. *Infant Potty Basics: With or Without Diapers, the Natural Way.* Lafayette, CO: White-Boucke Publishing, Inc., 2003.

Brooks, R. C., R. M. Copen, D. J. Cox, J. Morris, S. Borowitz, and J. Sutphen. "Review of the Treatment Literature for Encopresis, Functional Constipation, and Stool-Toileting Refusal." *Annals of Behavioral Medicine* 22 (2000): 260–67.

Issenman, Robert M., Robert Bruce Filmer, and Peter A. Gorski. "A Review of Bowel and Bladder Control Development in Children: How Gastrointestinal and Urological Conditions Relate to Problems in Toilet Training." *Pediatrics* 103 (1999): 1346–52.

Lansky, Vicki. *Toilet Training: A Practical Guide to Daytime and Nighttime Training.* Minnetonka, MN: Book Peddlers, 2002.

Partin, J. C., S. K. Hamill, J. E. Fischel, and J. S. Partin. "Painful Defecation and Fecal Soiling in Children." *Pediatrics* 89 (1992): 1007–9.

Schonwald, Alison, Lon Sherritt, Ann Stadtler, and Carolyn Bridgemohan. "Factors Associated with Difficult Toilet Training." *Pediatrics* 113 (2004): 1753–57.

Schum, Timothy R., T. L. McAuliffe, M. D. Simms, J. A. Walter, M. Lewis, and R. Pupp. "Factors Associated with Toilet Training in the 1990s." *Ambulatory Pediatrics* 1 (2001): 79–86.

Sears, Robert R., Eleanor E. Maccoby, and Harry Levin. *Patterns of Child Rearing.* New York City: Row, Peterson & Company, 1957.

Chapter 6

Bauer, Ingrid. *Diaper Free! The Gentle Wisdom of Natural Infant Hygiene.* Saltspring Island, British Columbia, Canada: Natural Wisdom Press, 2001.

Boucke, Laurie. *Infant Potty Basics: With or Without Diapers, the Natural Way.* Lafayette, CO: White-Boucke Publishing, Inc., 2003.

deVries, Marten W., and M. Rachel deVries. "Cultural Relativity of Toilet Training Readiness: A Perspective from East Africa." *Pediatrics* 60 (1977): 170–77.

Hellstrom, Anna-Lena. "Influence of Potty Training Habits on Dysfunctional Bladder in Children." *The Lancet* 356 (2000): 1787.

Leavitt, L. A. "Mothers' Sensitivity to Infant Signals." *Pediatrics* 102 (1998): 1247–49.

Schaefer, Charles E., and Theresa Foy DiGeronimo. *Toilet Training Without Tears*. New York City: Penguin Group, 1997.

Schum, Timothy R., T. L. McAuliffe, M. D. Simms, J. A. Walter, M. Lewis, and R. Pupp. "Factors Associated with Toilet Training in the 1990s." *Ambulatory Pediatrics* 1 (2001): 79–86.

Sears, Robert R., Eleanor E. Maccoby, and Harry Levin. *Patterns of Child Rearing*. New York City: Row, Peterson & Company, 1957.

Smeets, P. M., G. E. Lancioni, T. S. Ball, and D. S. Oliva. "Shaping Self-Initiated Toileting in Infants." *Journal of Applied Behavior Analysis* 18 (1985): 303–8.

Sun, M., and S. Rugolotto. "Assisted Infant Toilet Training in a Western Family Setting." *Journal of Developmental Behavioral Pediatrics* 25 (2004): 99–101.

Chapter 7

Bakker, E., and J. J. Wyndaele. "Changes in the Toilet Training of Children During the Last 60 Years: The Cause of an Increase in Lower Urinary Tract Dysfunction?" *British Journal of Urology* 86 (2000): 248–52.

Boucke, Laurie. *Infant Potty Basics: With or Without Diapers, the Natural Way*. Lafayette, CO: White-Boucke Publishing, Inc., 2003.

Schaefer, Charles E., and Theresa Foy DiGeronimo. *Toilet Training Without Tears*. New York City: Penguin Group, 1997.

Schonwald, Alison, Lon Sherritt, Ann Stadtler, and Carolyn Bridgemohan. "Factors Associated with Difficult Toilet Training." *Pediatrics* 113 (2004): 1753–58.

Schum, Timothy R., T. L. McAuliffe, M. D. Simms, J. A. Walter, M. Lewis, and R. Pupp. "Factors Associated with Toilet

Training in the 1990s." *Ambulatory Pediatrics* 1 (2001): 79–86.

Sears, Robert R., Eleanor E. Maccoby, and Harry Levin. *Patterns of Child Rearing*. New York City: Row, Peterson & Company, 1957.

Van Pelt, Katie. *Potty Training Your Baby*. New York City: Signet Books, 2002.

Chapter 8

Bakker, E. "Results of a Questionnaire Evaluating Different Aspects of Personal and Familial Situation, and the Methods of Potty-Training in Two Groups of Children with a Different Outcome of Bladder Control." *Scandinavian Journal of Urology and Nephrology* 35 (2001): 370–78.

Bakker, E., and J. J. Wyndaele. "Changes in the Toilet Training of Children During the Last 60 Years: The Cause of an Increase in Lower Urinary Tract Dysfunction?" *British Journal of Urology* 86 (2000): 248–52.

Bloom, D. A., W. W. Seeley, M. L. Ritchey, and E. J. McGuire. "Toilet Habits and Continence in Children: An Opportunity Sampling in Search of Normal Parameters." *Journal of Urology* 149 (1993): 1087–90.

Blum, Nathan J., Bruce Taubaum, and Nicole Nemeth. "Relationship Between Age at Initiation of Toilet Training and Duration of Training: A Prospective Study." *Pediatrics* 111 (2003): 810–14.

Gesell, Arnold. *Infant and Child in the Culture Today*. New York City: Harper & Row, 1943.

Hartman, Moshe. "Sex and Sociocultural Correlates of Urinary Incontinence in Israeli Preschool Children." *Journal of General Psychology* 123 (1996): 150–68.

Hellstrom, Anna-Lena. "Influence of Potty Training Habits on Dysfunctional Bladder in Children." *The Lancet* 356 (2000): 1787.

Herbert, Martin. *Toilet Training, Bedwetting, and Soiling.* London: The British Psychological Society, 1996.

Maizels, Max, Kevin Gandhy, Barbara Keating, and Diane Rosenbaum. "Diagnosis and Treatment for Children Who Cannot Control Urination." *Current Problems in Pediatrics* 10 (1993): 402–50.

Schum, Timothy R., T. L. McAuliffe, M. D. Simms, J. A. Walter, M. Lewis, and R. Pupp. "Factors Associated with Toilet Training in the 1990s." *Ambulatory Pediatrics*, 1 (2001): 79–86.

Seim, H. C. "Toilet Training in First Children." *Journal of Family Practice* 29 (1989): 633–36.

Chapter 9

Brazelton, T. Berry, and Joshua D. Sparrow. *Toilet Training the Brazelton Way.* Cambridge, MA: Da Capo Press, 2004.

Coughlin, Elizabeth C. "Assessment and Management of Pediatric Constipation in Primary Care." *Pediatric Nursing* 29 (2003): 296–301.

Hellstrom, Anna-Lena. "Influence of Potty Training Habits on Dysfunctional Bladder in Children." *The Lancet* 356 (2000): 1787.

Kawauchi, Akihiro, Yoshiyuki Tanaka, Yutaka Yamao, Mitsuhiko Inaba, Motohiro Kanazawa, Osamu Ukimura, Yoichi Mizutani, and Tsuneharu Miki. "Follow-Up Study of Bedwetting from 3 to 5 Years of Age." *Pediatric Urology* 58 (2001): 772–76.

Laino, Charlene. "Defecation Anxiety Linked to Functional Constipation in Children," Medscape Medical News, 2003, medscape.com. Accessed January 2005.

Neveus, T., J. Hetta, S. Cnattingius, T. Tuvemo, G. Lackgren, U. Olsson, and A. Stenberg. "Depth of Sleep and Sleep Habits Among Enuretic and Incontinent Children." *Acta Paediatric* 88 (1999): 748–52.

Polaha, Jodi, William J. Warzak, and Karen Dittmer-McMahon. "Toilet Training in Primary Care: Current Practice and Recommendations from Behavioral Pediatrics." *Journal of Developmental & Behavioral Pediatrics* 23 (December 2002): 424–29.

Schmitt, B. D. "Toilet Training Resistance." *Clinical Reference Systems* (2000): 1632.

Schmitt, Barton D. "Toilet Training: Getting It Right the First Time." *Contemporary Pediatrics* 21, no. 4 (2004): 105–8, 111, 112, 116, 120–22.

Chapter 10

American Psychiatric Association. *Diagnostic and Statistic Manual of Mental Disorders*, Fourth Edition. Washington, DC: American Psychiatric Association, 1994.

Bauer, Ingrid. *Diaper Free! The Gentle Wisdom of Natural Infant Hygiene*. Saltspring Island, British Columbia: Natural Wisdom Press, 2001.

Blum, Nathan J., Bruce Taubaum, and Nicole Nemeth. "Relationship Between Age at Initiation of Toilet Training and Duration of Training: A Prospective Study." *Pediatrics* 111 (2003): 810–14.

Boucke, Laurie. *Infant Potty Basics: With or Without Diapers, the Natural Way*. Lafayette, CO: White-Boucke Publishing, Inc., 2003.

Brazelton, T. Berry. *Touchpoints: The Essential Reference*. Reading, MA: Addison-Wesley Publishing Co., 1992.

Byrd, Robert S., M. Weitzman, N. E. Lanphear, and P. Auinger. "Bed-Wetting in US Children: Epidemiology and Related Behavior Problems." *Pediatrics* 98 (1996): 414–19.

Egger, J., C. H. Carter, J. F. Soothill, and J. Wilson. "Effect of Diet Treatment on Enuresis in Children with Migraine or Hyperkinetic Behavior." *Clinical Pediatrics* 31 (1992): 302–7.

Fergusson, D. M., B. A. Hons, L. J. Horwood, et al. "Factors Related to the Age of Attainment of Nocturnal Bladder Control: An 8-Year Longitudinal Study." *Pediatrics* 78 (1986): 884–90.

Issenman, Robert M., Robert Bruce Filmer, and Peter A. Gorski. "A Review of Bowel and Bladder Control Development in Children: How Gastrointestinal and Urological Conditions Relate to Problems in Toilet Training." *Pediatrics* 103 (1999): 1346–52.

Kaneko, K., S. Fujinaga, Y. Ohtomo, T. Shimizu, and Y. Yamashiro. "Combined Pharmacotherapy for Nocturnal Enuresis." *Pediatric Nephrology* 16 (2001): 662–64.

Kawauchi, Akihiro, Yoshiyuki Tanaka, Yutaka Yamao, Mitsuhiko Inaba, Motohiro Kanazawa, Osamu Ukimura, Yoichi Mizutani, and Tsuneharu Miki. "Follow-Up Study of Bedwetting from 3 to 5 Years of Age." *Pediatric Urology* 58 (2001): 772–76.

Maizels, Max. Happy bladder diet for children who wet, tryfordry .com/html/diet.htm. Accessed January 2005.

Maizels, Max, D. Rosenbaum, and B. Keating. *Getting to Dry: How to Help Your Child Overcome Bedwetting.* Boston: Harvard Common Press, 1999.

Neveus, T., J. Hetta, S. Cnattingius, T. Tuvemo, G. Lackgren, U. Olsson, and A. Stenberg. "Depth of Sleep and Sleep Habits Among Enuretic and Incontinent Children." *Acta Paediatric* 88 (1999): 748–52.

Pashankar, D. S., and W. P. Bishop. "Efficacy and Optimal Dose of Daily Polyethylene Glycol 3350 for Treatment of Constipation and Encopresis in Children." *Pediatrics* 139 (2001): 428–32.

Sears, Robert R., Eleanor E. Maccoby, and Harry Levin. *Patterns of Child Rearing*. New York City: Row, Peterson & Company, 1957.

Sears, William. Constipation, askdrsears.com/html/8/t081100 .asp. Accessed January 2005.

Taubman, Bruce. "Toilet Training and Toileting Refusal for Stool Only: A Prospective Study." *Pediatrics* 99 (1997): 54–58.

Timms, D. J. "Rapid Maxillary Expansion in the Treatment of Nocturnal Enuresis." *Angle Orthodontist* 60 (1990): 229–33.

Yuksek, M. S., A. F. Erdem, C. Atalay, and A. Demirel. "Acupressure Versus Oxybutinin in the Treatment of Enuresis." *The Journal of International Medical Research* 31 (2003): 552–56.

Appendix A

Azrin, Nathan H., and Richard M. Foxx. *Toilet Training in Less than a Day*. New York City: Simon & Schuster, 1974.

Bakker, Wilhelmina. *Research into the Influence of Potty-Training on Lower Urinary Tract Dysfunction*. Antwerp, Belgium: University of Antwerp, 2002.

Brooks, R. C., R. M. Copen, D. J. Cox, J. Morris, S. Borowitz, and J. Sutphen. "Review of the Treatment Literature for Encopresis, Functional Constipation, and Stool-Toileting Refusal." *Annals of Behavioral Medicine* 22 (2000): 260–67.

Foxx, Richard M., Nathan H. Azrin. *Toilet Training the Retarded: A Rapid Program for Day and Nighttime Independent Toileting*. Champaign, IL: Research Press, 1973.

Issenman, Robert M., Robert Bruce Filmer, and Peter A. Gorski. "A Review of Bowel and Bladder Control Development in Children: How Gastrointestinal and Urological Conditions

Relate to Problems in Toilet Training." *Pediatrics* 103 (1999): 1346–52.

Kuhn, B. R., B. A. Marcus, and S. L. Pitner. "Treatment Guidelines for Primary Nonretentive Encopresis and Stool Toileting Refusal." *American Family Physician* 59 (1999): 2171–78.

Partin, J. C., S. K. Hamill, J. E. Fischel, and J. S. Partin. "Painful Defecation and Fecal Soiling in Children." *Pediatrics* 89 (1992): 1007–9.

Sears, William. Constipation, askdrsears.com/html/8/t081100 .asp. Accessed January 2005.

Taubman, Bruce. "Toilet Training and Toileting Refusal for Stool Only: A Prospective Study." *Pediatrics* 99 (1997): 54–58.

Index